Performing Toys

Spiky Monster.
For instructions and further plates, see Pages 75-9

Performing Toys

Alice White

Taplinger Publishing Company
New York

OR 1/83

First Published 1970 in England
by Mills & Boon Limited,
17–19 Foley Street, WIA IDR.

First Published 1970 in the United States
by Taplinger Publishing Co., Inc.
New York, New York

British ISBN 0 263.51522.2
American ISBN 0–8008–6280–5

Library of Congress Number 72–126993

Third Printing

Acknowledgements

I wish to thank Miss M. Sadovsky, Headmistress of the County Primary School, Knotty Ash, Liverpool, for the wonderful co-operation I received from her and her staff and for enabling me to work with such delightful children. Also the students from St. Katharine's College of Education, Liverpool, who tried out some of the experiments in school and also made some of the Space-Age toys.

I am also grateful to Ian Sharp, Lecturer in Music at St. Katharine's College, Liverpool, for his contribution on suggestions of music suitable for use with the toys.

I wish to thank J. J. Corlett for silhouette illustrations and M. R. Corlett and C. Roberts for illustrations of Space-Age toys.

The following plates, 2, 5, 6, 9, 10, 12, 13, 19, 24, 26 and 27 were photographed by P. N. Harling.

Other plates and jacket picture by Alec Davis.

**Plate 1
and 1a
(overleaf)**   From odds and ends to the finished article. These
children show how absorbing and rewarding the
making of these toys can be

Contents

Introduction

A large variety of toys exists from soft cuddly toys to solid wooden ones, but there are some toys which have a real character of their own and become alive with the actions they make.

Some of the toys in this book have very interesting and individual characters and perform in a fascinating way. They can be made to move and dance, to sit, kneel, do exercises, go for walks, act plays together—I have not attempted to give detailed instructions about this, as there are so many possibilities, and the best way to discover them is just to play with the toys.

Many of them make little clinking and chattering noises (not *too* loud!); these are fun in themselves, but more so when linked up with rhythm and music. My colleague Ian Sharp has contributed a chapter about this, suggesting how parents or teachers can introduce a group of children to this type of play.

The toys can be easily designed and take upon themselves a personal character because of the materials used and the build-up of the shape. These toys appeal to all ages and are fascinating to make.

Performing Toys

Tools and equipment for the space-age toys

Scissors Pointed, with a 3-in. (8 cm.) blade.

Bradawl Wooden handle and sharp metal point, used for piercing holes in bottle tops. Fig. 1.

FIG. 1

Needles (Large eyes) 2 to 3 in. (5 to 6 cm.) in length.

Paste brush With 1-in. (3 cm.) bristles.

Paste Use powder paste (wallpaper type) but make up thickly like cream and place in a screw-top jar.
Used for sticking paper to balloons.

Adhesive Obtainable in tubes. Used for sticking sections of the toys together. Copydex and Bostik were used for the toys in this book, but virtually any good adhesive will do. (Elmer's Glue-All is suggested for U.S.A.).

String Must be thin. Used for threading legs and arms of toys on to body.

Thread Light-coloured, but must be strong. "Heavy-duty" suggested.
Used to suspend toys from rods when performing.

Silver Paint May be bought in aerosol cans, and applied by spraying. Directions on the cans should be carefully followed.

Materials

Almost any form of waste material can be used for performing toys, but those used for the toys illustrated in this book are as follows:

Egg boxes of various sizes and shapes (Plate 2, No. 1) or, as in Fig. 2a. The sections can be cut off as in Figs. 2b and 2c. A more rounded variety can be seen in Fig. 3a and when cut off they look like Figs. 3b and 3c. When eggs are purchased in large quantities, then the packing containers look like Plate 2, No. 1. The one container has had sections removed and so makes an attractive design. The sections removed are often stuck together in pairs, Fig. 14, Page 19. Great use is made of these shapes for the various toys.

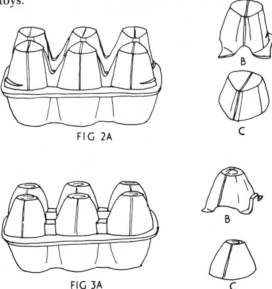

FIG 2A

B

C

FIG 3A

B

C

Plastic cartons, which have been used to contain cream, yoghurt, cheese, detergents, etc.

Tubes which have been used as centres of paper towels, toilet rolls (Plate 2, Nos. 4 and 5) or tubes which have

Plate 2   Materials that will be required with identifying key

been used for gift packing. These often have a transparent cylinder section. Metal tubes which have contained tablets, etc.

Bottle tops (Plate 2, Nos. 22 and 23), metal crown tops (caps) (No. 20), plastic caps from all kinds of containers, such as those found on tooth-paste tubes; cosmetic containers; detergent containers, etc. The tops may be very small or quite large. Screw-on metal caps.

Paper beakers (Plate 2, No. 15) or styrofoam coffee cups.

Balloons of all shapes and sizes.

Pipe cleaners, because they are pliable and easy to obtain.

Beads and buttons of all shapes and sizes are useful for spacing out sections, or for eyes, etc

1. Egg Carton
2. Cream Carton
3. Yoghurt Carton
4 and 5. Tubes (cardboard)
6. Plastic Bottle
7 and 8. Cartons
9. Cheese Box
10. Metal Screw-on Cap
11 and 12. Mousse or Ice-cream Moulds
13. Lids from Cartons
14. Egg Box
15. Paper Beaker
16. Plastic Bottle
17, 18 and 19. Cartons
20. Metal Bottle Tops (Caps)
21. Metal Screw-on Cap
22 and 23. Plastic Bottle Caps

Plate 3   Yo-Lek

14

Yo-Lek

Materials required   See Fig. 4.
String—2 pieces each 18 in. (46 cm.) long.

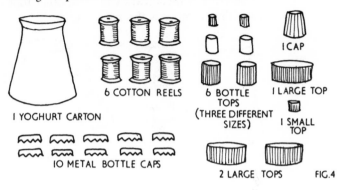

1 YOGHURT CARTON

6 COTTON REELS

6 BOTTLE TOPS (THREE DIFFERENT SIZES)

1 CAP

1 LARGE TOP

1 SMALL TOP

10 METAL BOTTLE CAPS

2 LARGE TOPS

FIG.4

Preparation Make holes in the centre of all bottle caps except the very small ones.

To make

A leg   Put a knot in the end of the string. Thread up through a large bottle top, then thread on three cotton spools, Fig. 5. Make a second leg.

Body   Make a hole on each side of yoghurt carton near the base, Fig. 6. Thread each leg string through the holes and tie in the centre, Fig. 7.

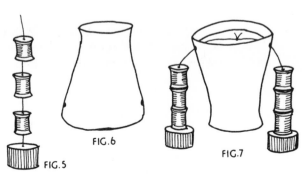

FIG.6

FIG.5

FIG.7

Arms   1. Put a knot at the end of the string, thread on three bottle tops of graded sizes, then four metal caps, Fig. 8.
2. Make a knot in the string then thread through the top holes of carton.
3. Make a knot in string near to the top edge of carton and thread on four metal caps and three other tops of graded sizes. This completes the arms, Fig. 9.

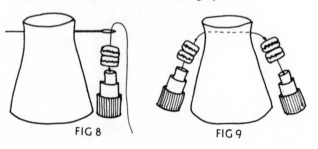

FIG 8   FIG 9

Head   1. Make two holes in opposite sides of large container top, Fig. 10.
2. Take a length of string, put a knot on the end, thread through a metal bottle cap and pass string through container and thread on another metal bottle cap, Fig. 11. Knot string firmly and cut off, Fig. 12.

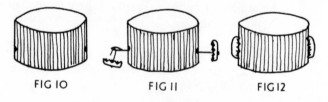

FIG 10   FIG 11   FIG 12

To attach head   Thread a length of string (end knotted) up through the base of body, Fig. 13, and through the head and a smaller bottle top, Fig. 13, stick firmly into position; also add a bottle top for nose.

To finish   Spray with silver paint.
Attach arms to a cross bar and body to a bar, see Page 85.

To make him perform   Raise arms or whole body and lower to the ground. This gives a bumping sound.

16

FIG13

17

Plate 4   Al-Lek

18

Al-Lek

Materials required See Fig. 14.
Three lengths of thin string, each 18 in. long (46 cm.).

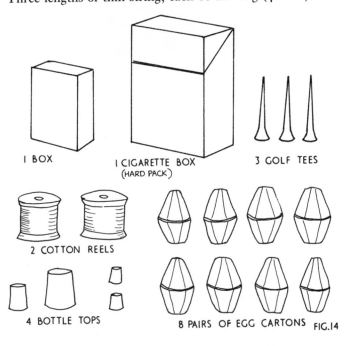

I BOX   I CIGARETTE BOX (HARD PACK)   3 GOLF TEES

2 COTTON REELS

4 BOTTLE TOPS   8 PAIRS OF EGG CARTONS   FIG.14

Preparation Using a bradawl make holes in the ends of egg-carton sections. Stick the carton sections together in pairs.

To make 1. Put a knot at the end of one length of string, then thread through a cotton spool and knot the string just above the reel, Fig. 15.
2. Thread a needle with the string. Pass needle through an egg-carton (previously stuck in pairs) and make a knot in the string just above the egg-carton, Fig. 16. Thread on a second egg-carton and make a knot, Fig. 17.
3. Make two holes in the base of cigarette box for the legs, and one hole in the top of box for the neck.
4. Pass the needle up through base of box and then through the top. This is one leg. Fig. 18.
5. Make a second leg and thread on to body.

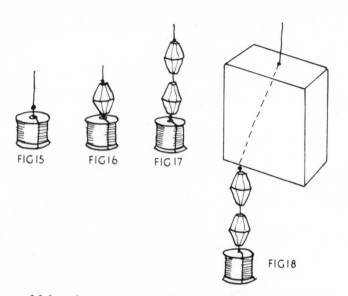

FIG 15   FIG 16   FIG 17

FIG 18

Arms

1. Make a knot on the end of string. Thread string through eye of needle and pass needle through egg-carton. Make a knot near to end of egg-carton. Thread on a second carton and make a knot, Fig. 19.

2. Make a hole through the sides of body near the top. Pass needle through this hole. Make a knot and continue threading on egg-cartons and making knots to complete second arm, Fig. 20. Leave top of box slightly open and stick firm with adhesive, Fig. 21.

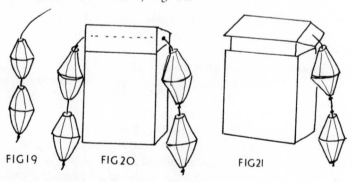

FIG 19   FIG 20   FIG 21

Head

Make a hole through the box from top to bottom. Using the two strings of the body as one, make two knots for neck, then thread on box for head. Make knot at top of head, Fig. 22.

20

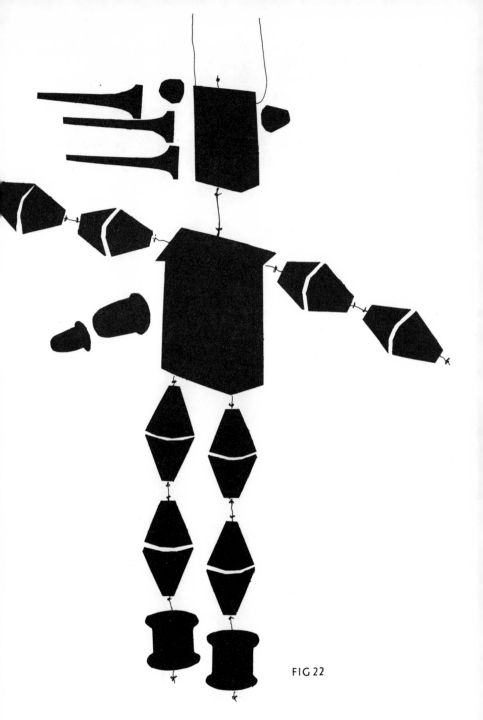

FIG 22

Stick on the two bottle tops to centre of body, then spray the whole with silver paint.

To finish, stick the three golf tees to front of face and the two bottle tops on to the side of head. Attach the two arms and the head section to pieces of wood as on Page 85.

To make him perform   Lift each arm section separately or together. This is a silent toy but the movement is attractive.

Jo-Lek

Materials
required

See Fig. 23.
String.

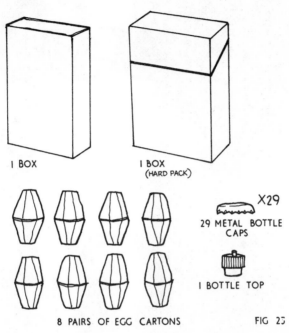

I BOX

I BOX
(HARD PACK)

X29

29 METAL BOTTLE
CAPS

I BOTTLE TOP

8 PAIRS OF EGG CARTONS

FIG 23

To make
Legs

1. Put a knot at end of string and thread up through four bottle caps, then make a knot in the string near to the caps, Fig. 24.
2. Thread on a pair of egg-cartons, then make a knot, Fig. 25.
3. Thread on two bottle caps and make a knot, Fig. 26. Then thread on a pair of egg-cartons. Make another knot near to cartons, Fig. 27. Make a second leg.

Body

Make two holes in base of larger box for legs and one in the top for neck. Also make two holes in the side for arms. Thread the leg strings up through the hole in the base and up through the neck. Put knot in string near to box, Fig. 28.

23

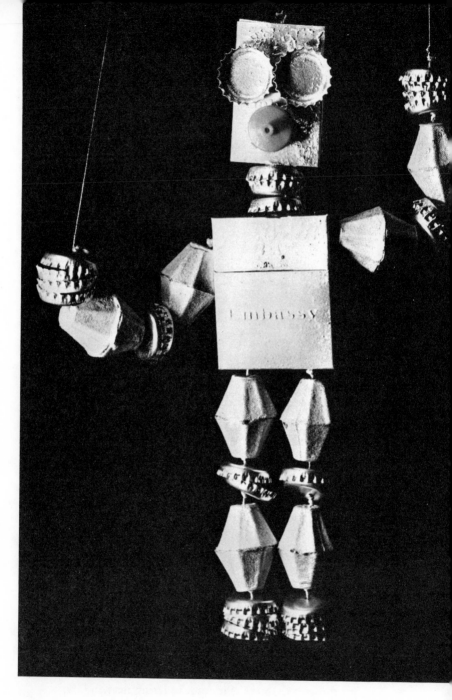

Plate 5 Jo-Lek

24

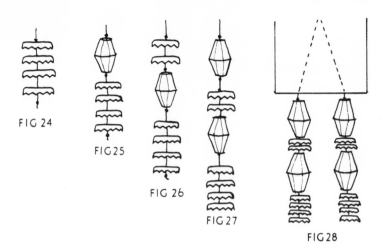

FIG 24

FIG 25

FIG 26

FIG 27

FIG 28

Arms

1. Make one arm as for leg.
2. Thread arm string through the box and put knot in string near to the box. Then thread on the pieces to make a second arm, Figs. 29 and 32.

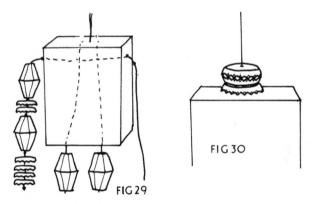

FIG 29

FIG 30

Neck and head

Thread on three bottle caps for neck and stick together with adhesive, Figs. 30 and 32.

Make a hole through the box from top to bottom and thread on smaller box for head. Make a knot at top of head. Stick on two bottle caps for eyes and stick on remaining top for nose, Fig. 31.

Spray with paint.

To finish, attach the arms and head to pieces of wood, see Page 85.

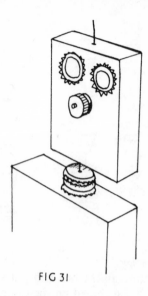

FIG 31

To make him perform   Raise each arm, or both, to obtain a tinkling sound. The legs also give an amusing sound effect if they are raised and lowered either quickly or slowly, according to the effect required.

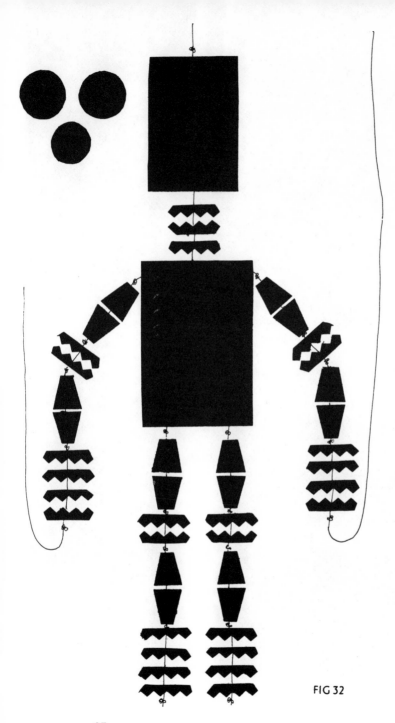

FIG 32

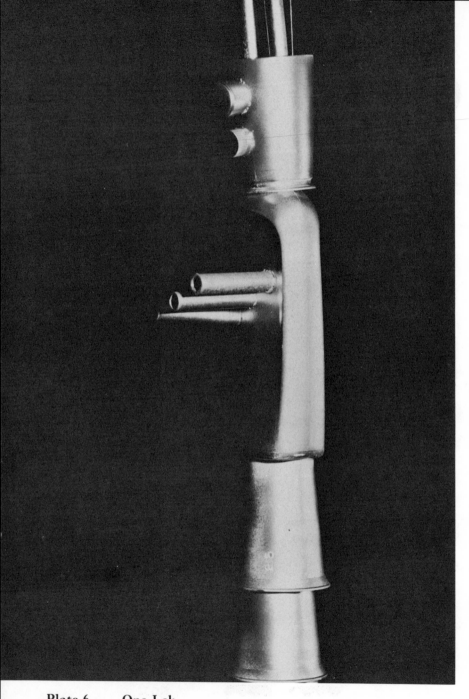

Plate 6   One-Lek

One-Lek

Materials required   See Fig. 33.
String.

3 PAPER CUPS

3 THIN TUBES

3 BUTTONS

2 SMALLER TUBES

2 BOTTLE TOPS

I YOGHURT CARTON

FIG. 33

I PLASTIC CONTAINER

Preparation Make a hole in the base of each paper cup and also in the bottom of the container. Also make a hole on each side of the top of the container.

To make 1. Thread a button on to the end of linen thread and secure into position by tying. Thread on a paper cup, Fig. 34. Pull thread tight.
2. Thread on a button and secure by a knot. The button should be 2 in. (5 cm.) from top of cup, Fig. 35. Thread on a second cup, then a button, and knot it into position 2 in. from the top of the previous cup. Thread on a third cup, Fig. 36.
3. Using a long needle, pass the end of the thread through the plastic container and up through a paper cup, Fig. 37.
4. Stick on the three thin tubes to the front of the container and the two short ones on to the top of the head. The two bottle tops are stuck on to the face.
A length of thread is passed down through the head close to one of the tubes and through the holes in the side of the container; then up through the yoghurt carton, Figs. 38 and 39.
Make sure that the three lengths of thread allow the cups forming the leg to remain extended and the head to rest on

29

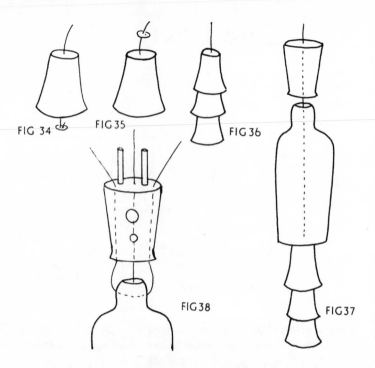

FIG 34   FIG 35   FIG 36   FIG 38   FIG 37

the container, then put adhesive around the threads at the top of the head to secure them.

To make him perform   Attach the three threads to a stick, Page 85, and raise and lower the toy to give it an interesting sound.

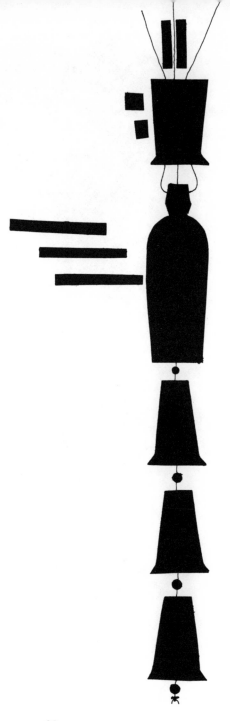

FIG 39

Plate 7   Tu-Lek

Tu-Lek

Materials required See Fig. 40. Two lengths of string each 24 in. (61 cm.) long.

I TOILET ROLL

STRIP OF CORRUGATED
FOAM PLASTIC
4"X6" (10 X 15 CM)

6 PAPER CUPS

2 HALF SECTIONS
OF EGG CARTONS

I SINGLE SECTION
OF EGG CARTON

3 SMALL
TUBES, ABOUT
I"LONG (3 CM)

3
PIPE CLEANERS

FRINGED BRAID ABOUT
18" (45 CM) LONG

I BOTTLE
TOP

I BOTTLE TOP

FIG. 40

Preparation Make a hole in base of each paper cup.

To make 1. Put a knot on the end of the string, and thread through hole in cup, Fig. 41.
2. Pull string tight, then make a knot 1 in. (2 cm.) above cup, Fig. 42.
3. Thread on second cup and make a knot as before, then thread on third cup, Fig. 43.

33

FIG 41   FIG 42   FIG 43

4. Make a second leg as previous one.

Body

1. Put one section of egg base flat, lay leg strings over it, Fig. 44. Stick so that legs are apart, A. Then stick strings together to form neck, B.

2. Place second egg section over the top and stick. Stick bottle top in the centre division near the top, Fig. 45.

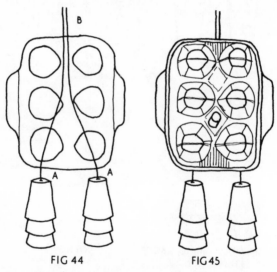

FIG 44   FIG 45

Head

Thread the two strings up through the single egg-carton section, Fig. 46. Thread string through toilet roll and stick egg-carton section to toilet roll, Fig. 47.

Cut off 2 in. (5 cm.) of fringed braid. Wind the rest of the braid tightly round the string (Fig. 48A) and stuff firmly into top of toilet roll, Fig. 48B. Wrap corrugated foam round toilet roll and stitch ends together, Fig. 49. For the features join two sections of corrugations together for eyes and below nose, Fig. 50.

34

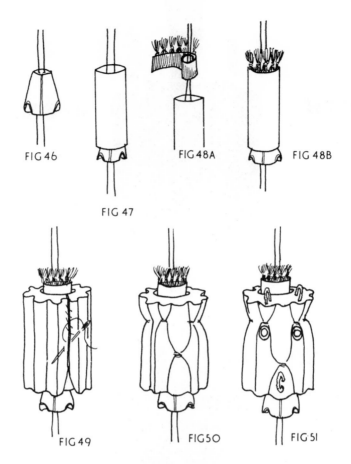

FIG 46   FIG 48A   FIG 48B

FIG 47

FIG 49   FIG 50   FIG 51

Spray with silver paint but leave legs white.
Complete features by pushing in pieces of tube for eyes.
Use pipe cleaner cut into small pieces and bent for the
mouth and for above eyes, Fig. 51.
The small piece of braid may be twisted tight and inserted
down the end of small tube and stuck on to the front of
the body.
If you cannot get corrugated foam, paper will do, but foam
is more fun.

**To make
him
perform**
Use a long length of thread attached to head so that the
toy can be raised and lowered. The sound effect is
obtained by this raising and lowering movement, whether
done quickly or slowly.

35

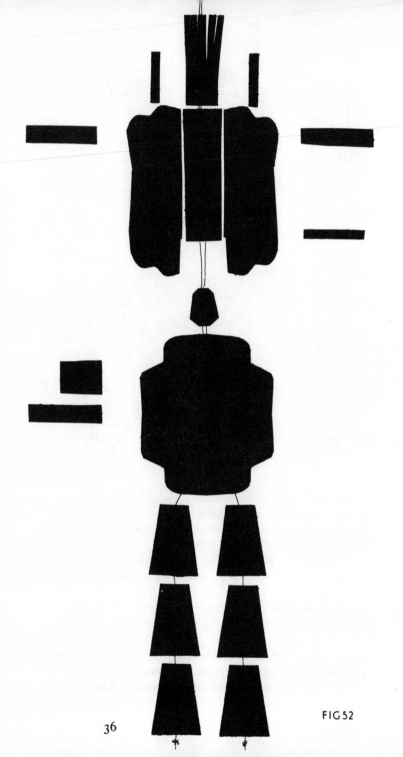

FIG 52

Wy-Aut

Materials
required
See Fig. 53.
String.
The polystyrene blocks come from the packing of
fluorescent light tubes.

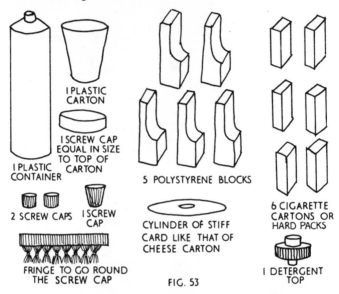

I PLASTIC
CARTON

I SCREW CAP
EQUAL IN SIZE
TO TOP OF
I PLASTIC   CARTON
CONTAINER

2 SCREW CAPS   I SCREW
CAP

FRINGE TO GO ROUND
THE SCREW CAP

5 POLYSTYRENE BLOCKS

CYLINDER OF STIFF
CARD LIKE THAT OF
CHEESE CARTON

FIG. 53

6 CIGARETTE
CARTONS OR
HARD PACKS

I DETERGENT
TOP

Preparation 1. Remove the inside of one cigarette carton, Fig. 54.
2. Push up the inside packing of one cigarette carton for
$\frac{1}{4}$ in. (5 mm.).
3. Spray all the cigarette packets, also plastic carton and
container and cylinder of stiff cardboard, with silver paint.

To make 1. Attach the legs to the polystyrene blocks, as in
Figs. 56 and 57.
2. For the arms, stick the cigarette packets to the thin
side of the polystyrene blocks, Fig. 58.
3. Cut one polystyrene block in two, Fig. 59A and B.
Stick one half to the side of the carton, Fig. 60, and stick
the other half to the opposite side.
4. Stick the fringe to the inside edge of the plastic screw
top, Fig. 61.
5. Attach two screw caps to carton for eyes. Fig. 60.

37

Plate 8   Wy-Aut

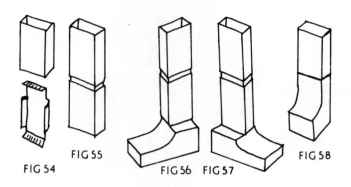

FIG 54 FIG 55 FIG 56 FIG 57 FIG 58

6. Stick the detergent top to the screw cap for nose,
Fig. 60, and attach to the carton.

7. Thread the pieces together as in Figs. 62 or 63.

Note: One long thread should pass up through the base of
the plastic container and on through the top of the
head, which should then be stuck onto the body,
Fig. 63.

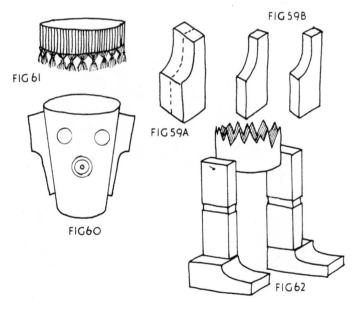

FIG 61 FIG 59B FIG 59A FIG 60 FIG 62

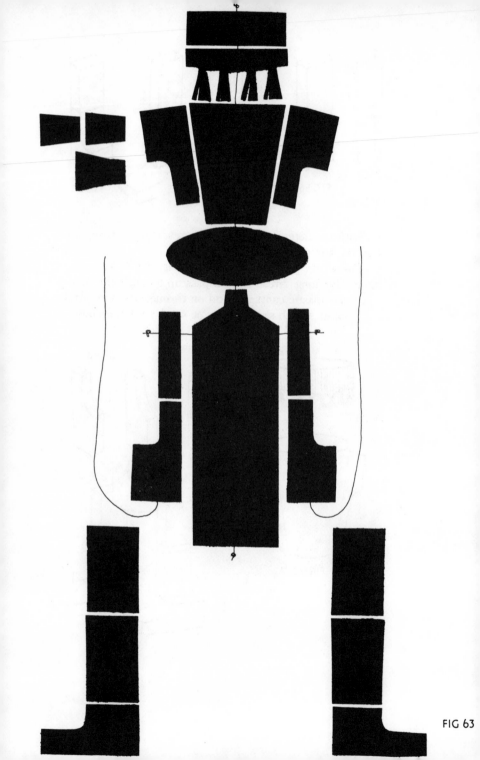

FIG 63

Gi-Lek

(So called because he is taller than the other toys and can be considered a giant.)

Materials required   See Fig. 64. Two lengths of thread each 48 in. long (122 cm.).

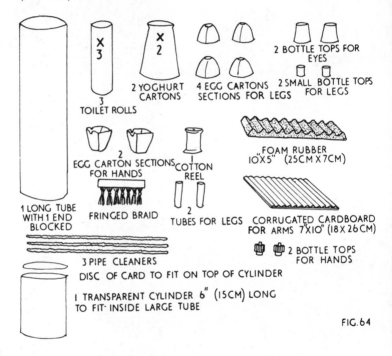

2 BOTTLE TOPS FOR EYES

2 SMALL BOTTLE TOPS FOR LEGS

X 3

X 2

3 TOILET ROLLS

2 YOGHURT CARTONS

4 EGG CARTONS SECTIONS FOR LEGS

2 EGG CARTON SECTIONS FOR HANDS

COTTON REEL

FOAM RUBBER 10"X5" (25CM X 7CM)

1 LONG TUBE WITH 1 END BLOCKED

FRINGED BRAID

2 TUBES FOR LEGS

CORRUGATED CARDBOARD FOR ARMS 7"X10" (18 X 26CM)

3 PIPE CLEANERS

2 BOTTLE TOPS FOR HANDS

DISC OF CARD TO FIT ON TOP OF CYLINDER

1 TRANSPARENT CYLINDER 6" (15CM) LONG TO FIT INSIDE LARGE TUBE

FIG. 64

To make

Legs   1. Stick a strip of fringed braid to the inside edge of an egg-carton, Fig. 65A and B.
2. Place second egg-carton on top, Fig. 65C.
3. Stick a small bottle top on to yoghurt carton, Fig. 66.
4. Using a long length of thread with knot on the end, pass thread through the egg-cartons and stick the cartons to bottle top, Fig. 67.
5. Thread on a small tube, also a toilet-roll tube (the two ends of which should be covered by two discs of card), Fig. 68.
Make a second leg.

41

Plate 9   Gi-Lek

42

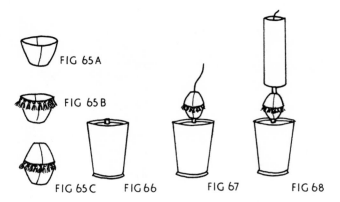

FIG 65A

FIG 65B

FIG 65C FIG 66 FIG 67 FIG 68

Arms

1. Thread on bottle top, then egg-carton (which has been previously cut as in Fig. 69C). The egg-carton should be stuck, Fig. 69D.
2. Join a strip of corrugated cardboard to form a tube and stick on a strip of fringed braid. Thread this on to previous section, Fig. 70. Make second arm in the same way.

Face

1. Stick buttons on to bottle tops and pass a pipe cleaner through one toilet-roll tube, which should be covered in brightly coloured paper, Fig. 71A and B.
2. Cover cotton spool with gilt paper and attach to tube with a pipe cleaner, Fig. 71C.

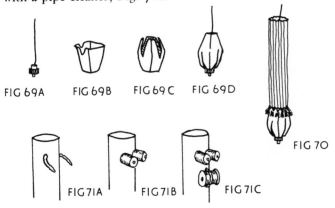

FIG 69A FIG 69B FIG 69C FIG 69D

FIG 71A FIG 71B FIG 71C

FIG 70

To make up

1. Thread leg threads up through the large tube.
2. Thread arm threads through large tube. Knot ends together on outside of tube, Fig. 72A.
3. Spray with silver paint.

43

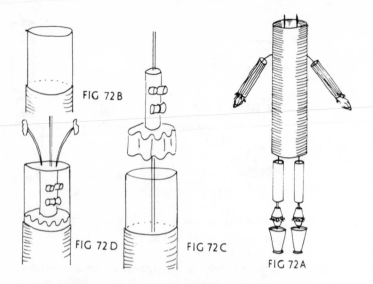

FIG 72B

FIG 72D

FIG 72C

FIG 72A

4. Place part of the clear plastic cylinder inside the body cylinder, allowing it to be visible for about 5 in. (13 cm.). Fig. 72B.

5. Wrap the foam rubber around the face cylinder, Fig. 72C (but first bring through the two long threads up the head) and press down gently into plastic cylinder so that about 1 in. of foam is showing. See plate 9.

6. Stick the outer disc of tube into position and put two pipe cleaners with strips of foam rubber at ends to form antennae, Fig. 72D.

To make him perform

Attach head and arm as on page 85. This toy does not make such an interesting sound but the scale of it gives the other toys greater interest.

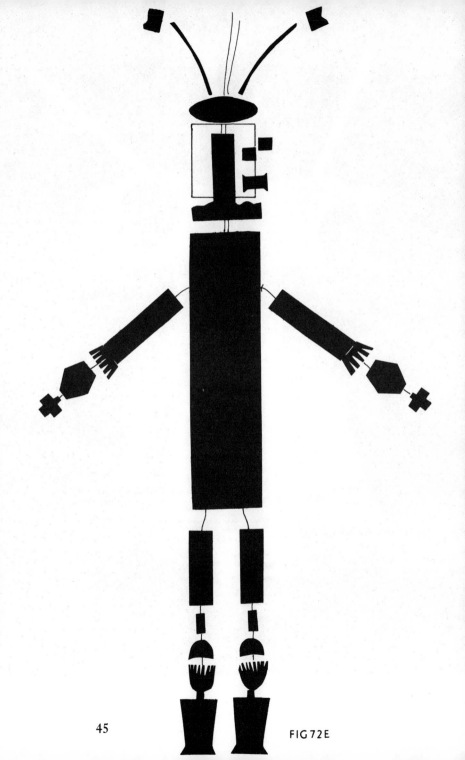

45   FIG 72E

Plate 10   Mini-Lek

Mini-Lek

With eyes all round its head, this sociable creature seems alert to everything that is going on.

Materials required See Fig. 73.
Four lengths of black thread each 20 in. (50 cm.) long. scrap of coloured nylon or tissue paper.

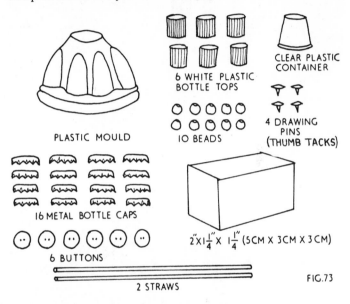

PLASTIC MOULD

6 WHITE PLASTIC BOTTLE TOPS

CLEAR PLASTIC CONTAINER

10 BEADS

4 DRAWING PINS (THUMB TACKS)

16 METAL BOTTLE CAPS

6 BUTTONS

$2'' \times 1\frac{1}{4}'' \times 1\frac{1}{4}''$ (5CM X 3CM X 3CM)

2 STRAWS

FIG.73

Preparation Spray the mould and box with silver paint.
Make a hole in the centre of the metal bottle caps.

To make
Legs 1. Thread a bead on to the end of black thread and secure with a knot, Fig. 74A.
2. Thread the thread through from the underside of a bottle cap, Fig. 74B.
3. Thread on a total of four caps, Fig. 74C.
4. Take a second piece of thread and repeat from Stage 1. Repeat with the third and fourth pieces of thread.

To make up 1. Make a hole, using the bradawl, in the base of the mould, Fig. 75. Do this in the four quarters, Fig. 76.

47

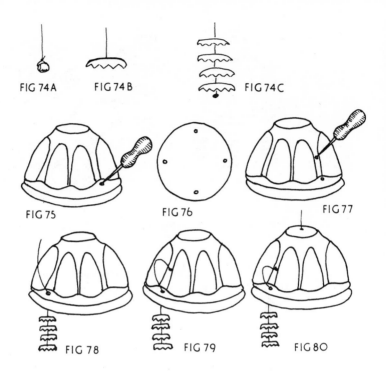

FIG 74A   FIG 74B   FIG 74C

FIG 75   FIG 76   FIG 77

FIG 78   FIG 79   FIG 80

2. Make four holes in the sides of the mould about $\frac{1}{4}$ in. up from previous hole, Fig. 77.

3. Make a hole in the top of the mould.

4. Make a hole in the top of the clear plastic container.

**To attach
Legs**

Thread the end of black thread into a needle and pass up through the mould, Fig. 78, then through the hole in the side, Fig. 79. Continue up through the hole in the top of the mould.

This completes one leg, Fig. 80.

Thread on all four legs.

A variation is to thread only three bottle caps onto one of the legs—this makes its movements even more comical, as if it had a will of its own and wouldn't always do what was expected of it.

Neck

Pass all four threads through the centre hole in the clear plastic container, Fig. 81.

49

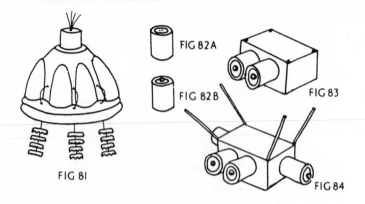

FIG 82A

FIG 82B

FIG 83

FIG 81

FIG 84

Put the coloured nylon into the neck and secure to body with adhesive.

Head

1. Stick a button on to the top of each white bottle top, then a bead into the centre of each button, Fig. 82A and B. These are for the eyes.

2. Make a hole in each of four corners of the box, Fig. 83.

3. Cut the straws into half and insert at the corners. Secure with adhesive, Fig. 84. Put a drawing pin or thumb tack at the end of each straw, securing with adhesive.

4. Stick an eye at each end of the box and two eyes on each long side, Figs. 83 and 84.

5. Make a hole in the centre of the box and pass the four ends of thread up through the hole. Then stick the box to the plastic container to complete the toy, Fig. 85.

To make it perform Raise and lower the toy gently to music and gradually increase the speed to obtain interesting leg movements and sound.

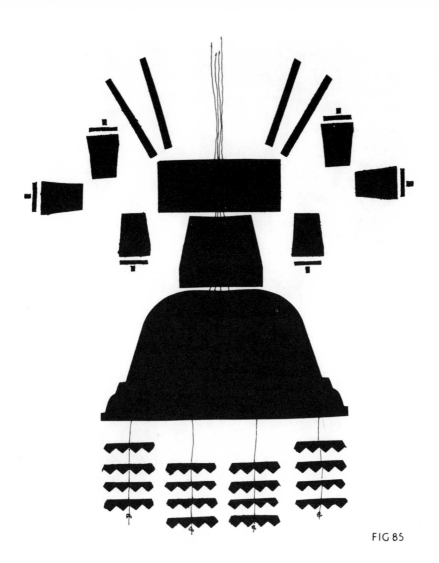

FIG 85

Plate 11   Dancing Top

A Dancing Top

Materials required
See Fig. 86.
Six lengths of black thread, each 20 in. (50 cm.) long.

PLASTIC MOULD

2 BOTTLE TOPS

18 METAL BOTTLE CAPS

DOME SHAPED TOP OF A CONTAINER

7 BEADS

FIG. 86

Preparation Spray the mould with silver paint.

To make
Legs See Page 47 instructions 1–4, but use only three bottle
caps for each leg.

To make 1. Make a hole (using the bradawl) in the base of the
up mould, Fig. 87.
2. Do this in the six sections, Fig. 88.
3. Make six holes in the sides of the mould at the top
of each section (about $\frac{1}{4}$ in. or 1·5 cm.), Fig. 89.
4. Make a hole in the top of the two remaining bottle
caps, also in dome-shaped top.
See page 47.

To attach
legs Pass all threads through a bead and knot the threads to
the bead, but leave the legs hanging loose, about $\frac{1}{4}$ in.
(or 0·5 cm.) below base, Fig. 90.

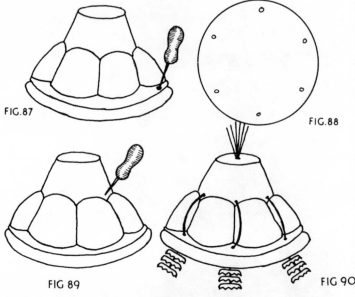

FIG.87

FIG.88

FIG 89

FIG 90

To Pass all six threads up through the centre hole in the large
complete bottle top, Fig. 91, then through the smaller one, Fig. 91.
Pass the threads up through the dome, Fig. 91.
Attach all sections together with adhesive.

54

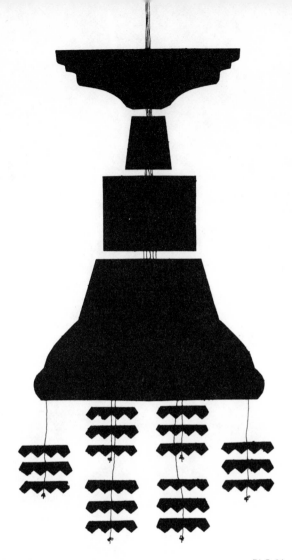

FIG 91

To make him perform   Use the group of threads as one thread. Raise and lower the body slightly, the legs remaining on the ground. This gives a clicking sound. Gradually raise and lower the whole toy and the sounds obtained will vary according to the height raised and the speed of operation.
This toy can glide, making a gentle sound, or it can become very much alive.

Plate 12   Mini-Creature

56

Mini-Creature

Materials See Fig. 92.
required Strong thread.

CREAM CARTON

2 BOTTLE TOPS

2 METAL
BOTTLE CAPS

2 PIPE CLEANERS

THIN TUBE

3"(8CM) BRAID WITH FRINGE

2 METAL TOPS WITH
STRAIGHT EDGES

FIG.92

To make 1. Make two holes in the top of each of the two serrated-edged bottle caps and a hole in opposite sides of cream carton (or yoghurt container), Figs. 93 and 94.
2. Take a length of thread and bring thread out through the side of the carton, pass through bottle cap and bring end back through hole in side of carton, Fig. 95. Thread on second bottle cap in the same way, tie ends of thread together inside carton, Fig. 96.

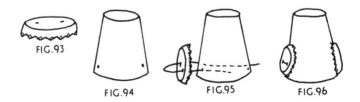

FIG.93

FIG.94

FIG.95

FIG.96

3. Make two holes in top of cream carton, one at each side, Fig. 97. Pass pipe cleaner through hole and down again to form a loop, twist ends together inside carton, Fig. 98.

57

4. Stick bottle top upwards on to top of carton, Fig. 99. Stick fringe to the other bottle top and place inside the previous one. Stick into position, Fig. 100.

5. Cut the tube into three pieces and paint silver. Stick two pieces of tube inside bottle caps for eyes. Stick the tube for eyes and nose on to cream carton, Figs. 101A and 101B. See also Fig. 102.

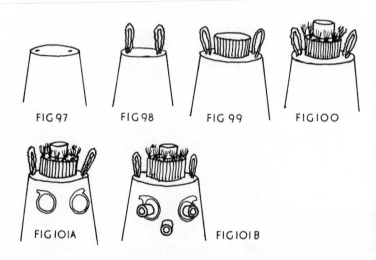

FIG 97   FIG 98   FIG 99   FIG 100

FIG 101A   FIG 101B

To make him perform   Attach two lengths of fine thread to pipe cleaner loops and then attach opposite ends to a stick. Move the toy by gliding, or raising and lowering.

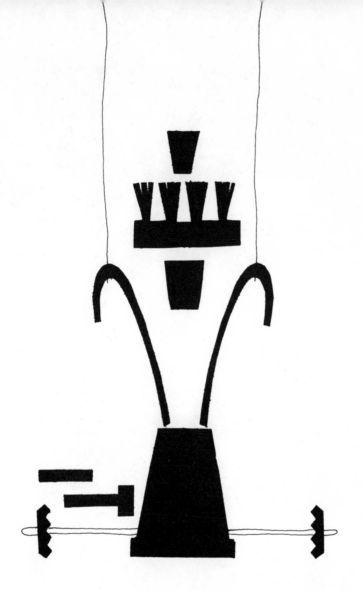

FIG 102

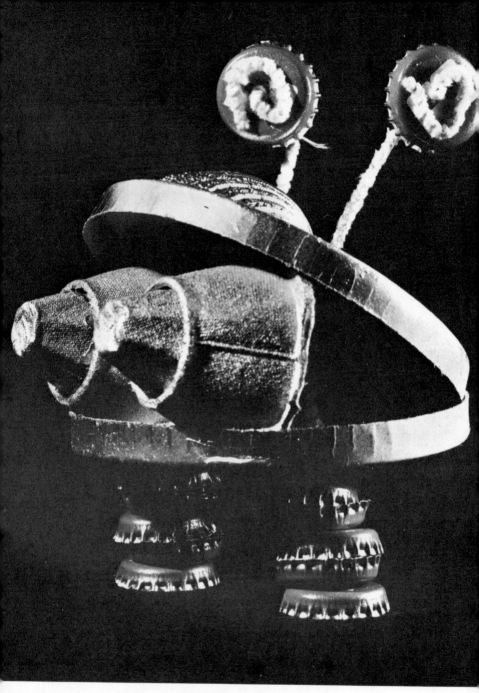

Plate 13   Large-eyed Mini-Creature

60

Large-eyed Mini-Creature

Materials required
See Fig. 103.
Two pieces string each 6 in. (16 cm.) long.

I CHEESE BOX

X14

14 METAL BOTTLE CAPS

I SHELL

2 SMALL SECTIONS OF EGG CARTONS

2 PIPE CLEANERS

SECTION OF EGG CARTON
FIG. 103

To make
1. Put knot on end of string and thread on six bottle caps, Fig. 104. Make a second leg in the same way.
2. Make two holes in the base of cheese box for legs.
3. Thread leg strings up through the holes and knot, Fig. 105.
4. Pass a pipe cleaner part way down each hole, Fig. 106.

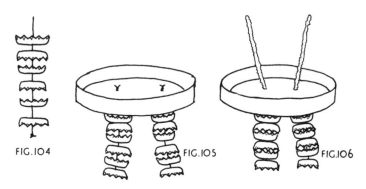

FIG.104   FIG.105   FIG.106

5. Make eyes by sticking a small egg-carton section on to each of the large egg-carton sections, Fig. 107.

6. Make two holes in the lid of box so that pipe cleaner can be pushed through from base.

7. Insert eye-section to keep box open and stick into position, Fig. 108.

8. Thread two bottle caps on to ends of pipe cleaners and stick shell into position, Fig. 109.

Spray silver.

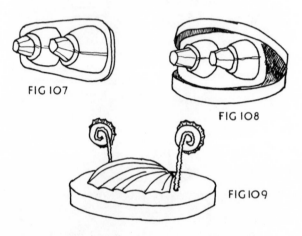

FIG 107

FIG 108

FIG 109

To make him perform   Tie long ends of linen thread to top of antennae and to a strip of wood. Raise and lower the toy, lifting up from the ground and lowering it, so that the legs make an interesting sound. Lift slowly, or quickly, to obtain the best sound effects.

FIG 110

Plate 14   **Wide-mouthed Mini-Creature**

Wide-mouthed Mini-Creature

Materials required   See Fig. 111.

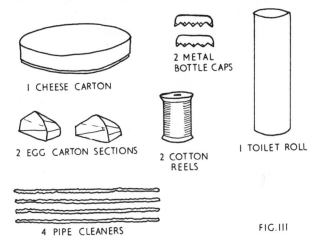

1 CHEESE CARTON

2 METAL BOTTLE CAPS

2 EGG CARTON SECTIONS

2 COTTON REELS

1 TOILET ROLL

4 PIPE CLEANERS

FIG.III

To make   1. Make four holes in base of box to equal width of cotton spools, Fig. 112.
2. Thread a cotton spool on to pipe cleaner, pass pipe cleaner up through the base of box, Fig. 113. Do the same with the other cotton spool.
3. Cut down the toilet roll, then cut off bands to equal $\frac{1}{2}$ in. (1 cm.), Figs. 114 and 115.

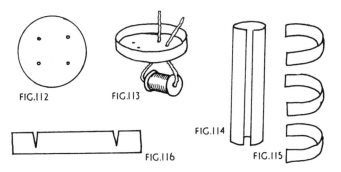

FIG.112   FIG.113

FIG.114

FIG.116

FIG.115

4. Make notches half way down the sides of the bands, Fig. 116, and arrange to form four loops on lower section of box and three on the top section, Figs. 117 and 119A.

5. Stick the top and bottom sections of the box together at the back.

6. Stick on egg-carton portions for eyes, with metal bottle caps inside. Thread a pipe cleaner through the back section of each egg-carton and bend into shape, Fig. 118.

Spray with paint before putting on the bottle caps.

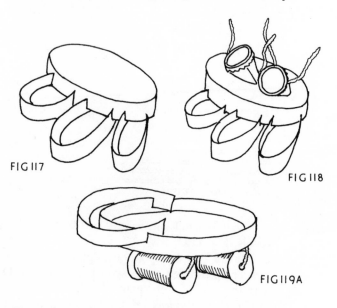

FIG 117

FIG 118

FIG 119A

To make him perform   Tie fine thread to ends of pipe cleaner and attach to stick, Page 85. This toy will glide and not make a noise.

FIG 119 B

Plate 15   Cylindrical Glider

Cylindrical Glider

**Materials
required**   See Fig. 120.

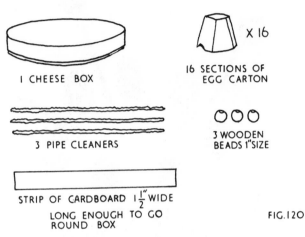

1 CHEESE BOX

X 16

16 SECTIONS OF
EGG CARTON

3 PIPE CLEANERS

3 WOODEN
BEADS 1"SIZE

STRIP OF CARDBOARD 1$\frac{1}{2}$"WIDE
LONG ENOUGH TO GO
ROUND BOX

FIG.120

To make   1. Stick the strip of cardboard round the bottom of the box, Fig. 121, then stick the lid on, Fig. 122.
2. Stick seven egg-carton sections on to the outer edge of top of the box, Fig. 123, and stick nine sections around the sides, Figs. 125 and 126. Spray with paint.
3. Thread a bead on to end of pipe cleaner and bend opposite end of pipe cleaner to form a ring, Fig. 124. Stick to the top of the lid. Use the two remaining cleaners and beads for two more antennae and stick in position.

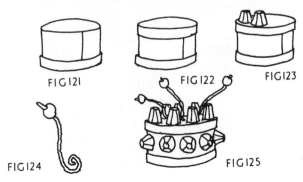

FIG 121

FIG 122

FIG 123

FIG 124

FIG 125

69

To make
him
perform

Make a hole through from top of box to underside and thread a length of fine thread through hole. Secure to underside of box with a knot. This toy will glide only, and not make a noise.

FIG 126

Monster

Though this and the next two monsters contain a lot of parts, they are well worth the trouble of collecting and making up.

Materials required
See Fig. 127.
Strong thread, paste and newspaper.

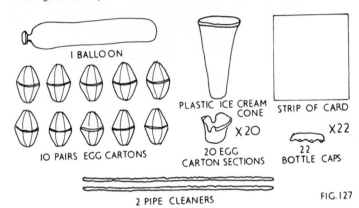

I BALLOON

PLASTIC ICE CREAM CONE

STRIP OF CARD

×20

×22

IO PAIRS EGG CARTONS

20 EGG CARTON SECTIONS

22 BOTTLE CAPS

2 PIPE CLEANERS

FIG. 127

To make
Legs

1. Use a short length of thread and thread on a metal bottle cap, Fig. 128A.
2. Thread on a pair of egg-carton sections, Fig. 128B.
3. Complete the leg by threading on another bottle cap, Fig. 128C. Make ten legs in all.

To make up

1. Blow up balloon and cover with five or six layers of paste and paper (torn small). Leave to dry.
2. Cut the egg-cartons into a more even shape, Fig. 129A and B.

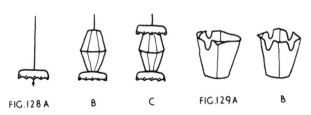

FIG.128 A   B   C   FIG.129A   B

Plate 16   Monster

3. Stick a row of four egg-cartons on to the balloon, then another row, Fig. 130.

4. Put a total of four rows on to the balloon.

5. Make the head by sticking four egg-cartons close together to form a solid shape. Then insert the cone in the spaces left, Fig. 131.

6. Stick two pipe cleaners into the two upper egg-cartons and attach bottle caps to these pipe cleaners, Figs. 131 and 135.

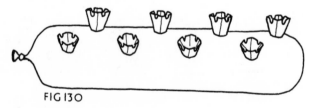

FIG 130

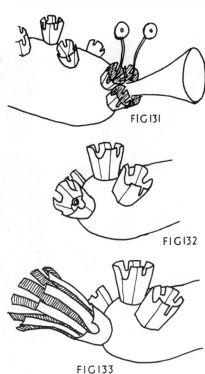

FIG 131

FIG 132

FIG 133

7. The tail is an egg-carton section and the card is cut into $\frac{1}{2}$-in. (1-cm.) wide strips and stuck to the inside of egg-carton, Figs. 132 and 133.

8. Stick on the legs to form two rows of five, Figs. 134 and 135.

Spray with silver paint.

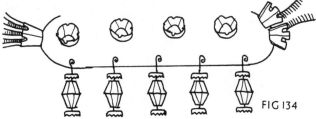

FIG 134

To make him perform   Attach monster to a stick, Page 85. The monster can be made to appear to walk by gradually moving it slowly along the ground; or it can be made to jump about by raising and lowering it quickly.

73

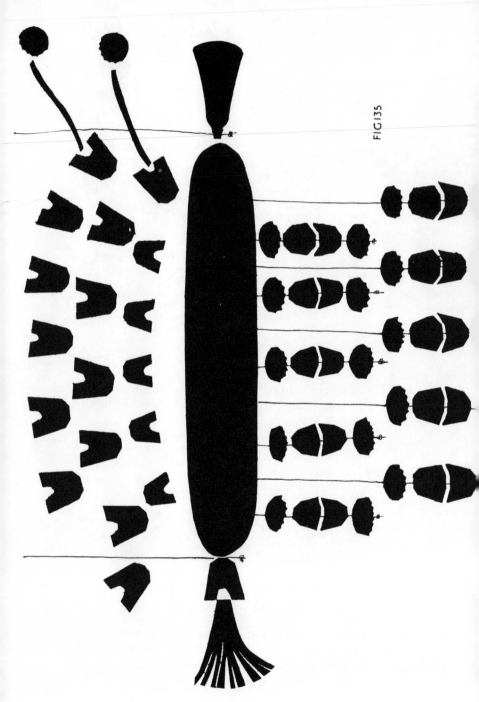

FIG 135

74

Spiky Monster

Plate 17   Spiky Monster

Materials required   See Fig. 136.
String, paste. Newspaper.

Preparation Blow up balloon and cover with several layers of paper, pasted one layer on top of the previous one. Leave to dry.

To make

Legs   1. Take a length of string and put a knot in the end; thread up through a metal bottle cap. Then thread through an egg-carton section, Fig. 137A. Stick this to the bottle cap but first put two wooden beads inside to form a rattle.
2. Thread on a second and third egg-carton section, Fig. 137B and C.

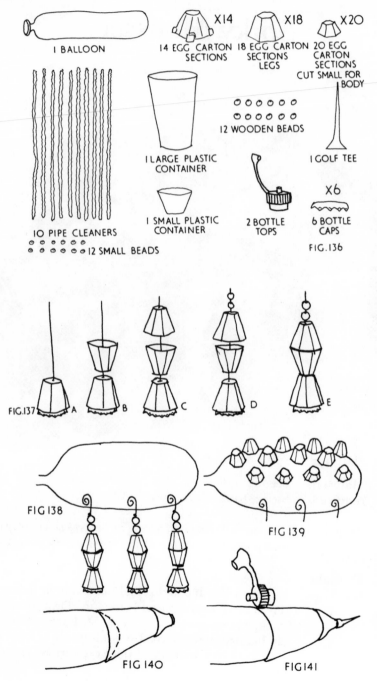

I BALLOON

14 EGG CARTON SECTIONS ×14

18 EGG CARTON SECTIONS LEGS ×18

20 EGG CARTON SECTIONS CUT SMALL FOR BODY ×20

12 WOODEN BEADS

I LARGE PLASTIC CONTAINER

I GOLF TEE

I SMALL PLASTIC CONTAINER

2 BOTTLE TOPS

6 BOTTLE CAPS ×6

IO PIPE CLEANERS

12 SMALL BEADS

FIG.136

FIG.137 A B C D E

FIG 138

FIG 139

FIG 140

FIG 141

3. Thread on two beads, Fig. 137D and E.
This completes one leg. Make six legs in all.

Body   1. Attach the legs to the body by sticking the string, close to the beads, on to the balloon, Fig. 138.
2. Stick the smaller egg-carton sections in five rows of four to the body, Fig. 139.

Head   Attach the large plastic container to the one end of the balloon, using adhesive. Add on the smaller container, then the golf tee, Figs. 140 and 141.

Tail   Thread 14 egg-carton sections on to a length of string, putting a knot after each section, Fig. 142A. Stick tail to end of balloon, Fig. 142B. Spray with silver paint and stick on two bottle tops for eyes, Fig. 141.

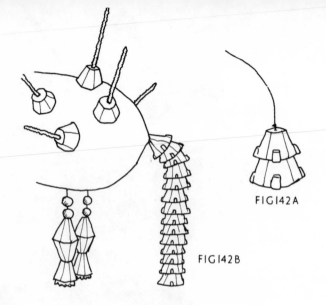

FIG 142 A

FIG 142 B

Cut the pipe cleaners into equal lengths and make a small
hole in each egg-carton section on the body and push end
of pipe cleaner into the hole.

Attach head and rear to a stick (Page 85).

To make   Raise and lower to obtain a sound effect.
him
perform

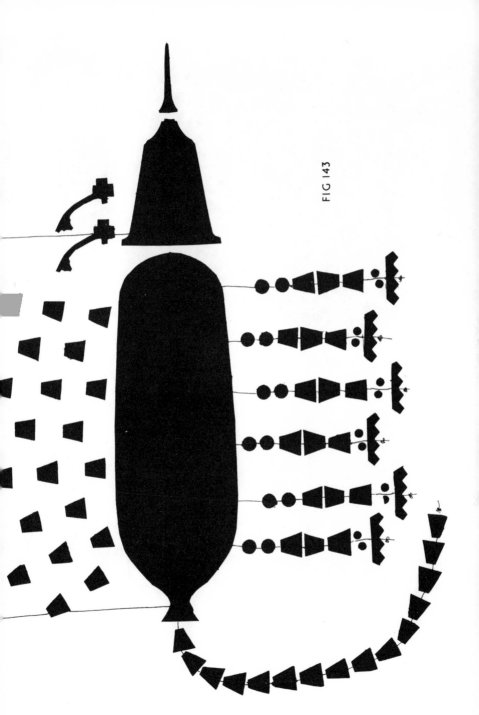

FIG 143

79

Plate 18   Rustling Monster

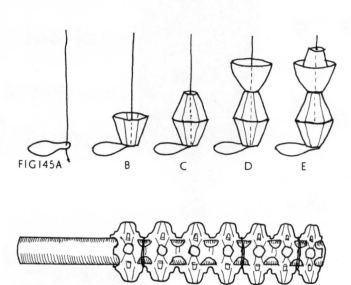

FIG 145 A   B   C   D   E

FIG 146

Rustling Monster

Materials required

See Fig. 144.

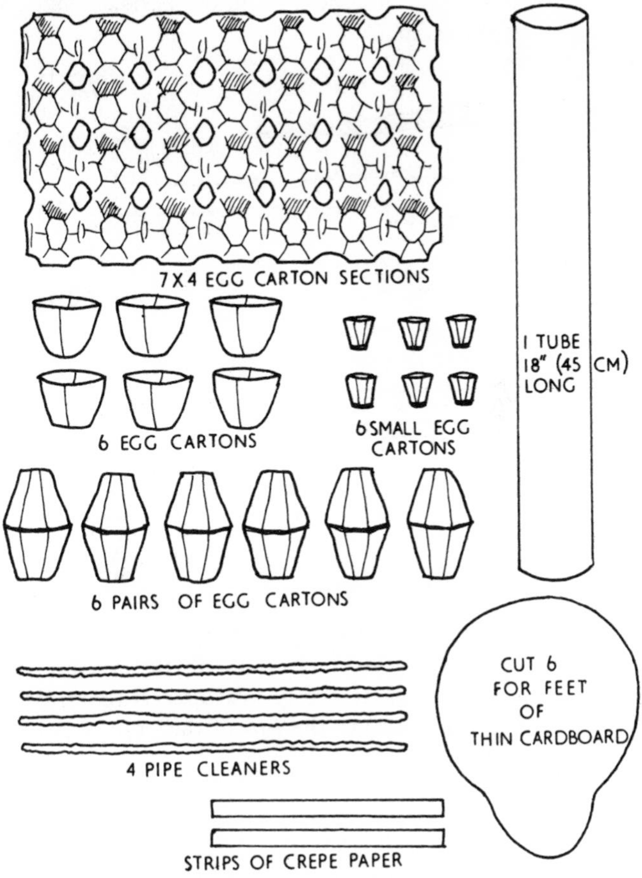

7 X 4 EGG CARTON SECTIONS

6 EGG CARTONS

6 SMALL EGG CARTONS

1 TUBE 18" (45 CM) LONG

6 PAIRS OF EGG CARTONS

4 PIPE CLEANERS

CUT 6 FOR FEET OF THIN CARDBOARD

STRIPS OF CREPE PAPER

FIG. 144

To make
Legs

1. Put a knot on the end of a length of thread and thread on a foot, Fig. 145A.
2. Thread on four egg-carton sections, Fig. 145B, C, D and E. Secure with adhesive. Make a total of six legs.

To make up

1. Wrap the egg-carton sections round the tube, Fig. 146, hold in place with thread wrapped round and tied; also use adhesive.

81

2. Cut down the tube to form $\frac{1}{2}$-in. (1-cm.) wide strips, Fig. 147. Stick pipe-cleaners on to the back of four strips so that they can be bent upwards. This end is the monster's head.

3. Stick three legs into position, Fig. 148, and the remaining three legs on to the opposite side. Spray with silver paint.

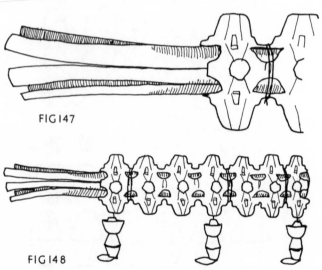

FIG 147

FIG 148

4. Cut the crepe paper into $\frac{1}{2}$-in. (1-cm.) wide strips. Stick long lengths inside top of tube for tail, Fig. 149, and also short lengths to the egg-cartons on the underside of body, Fig. 149. Also to the tips of the prongs of the head, Fig. 149.

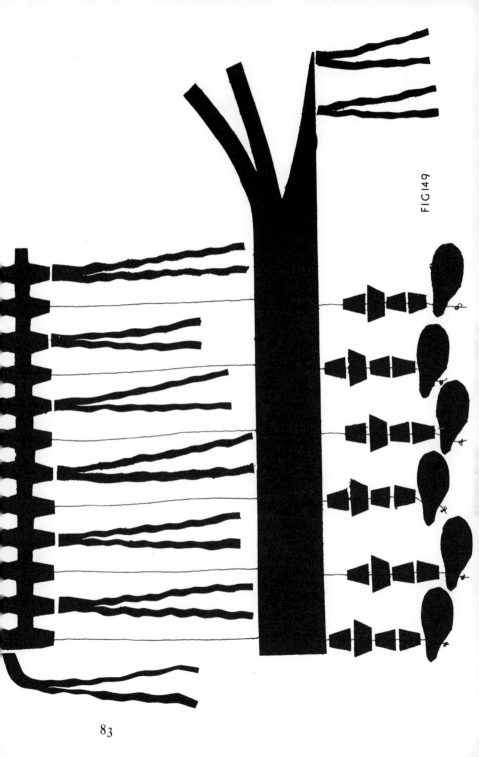

FIG 149

Movement and sounds

The toys must first be attached to a stick so that they can be raised or lowered.

First make a cross-bar from two pieces of thin wood. The length of each may be 4 in. (10 cm.). Stick or nail together.

The string or thread which comes out of the top of the toy, Fig. 150, is attached to the centre of the cross-bar as in Fig. 150.

For a Space Man, attach the string at the top of the toy to the cross-bar, then lay the toy flat; take a straight piece of wood and place this well below the feet, 18 to 24 in. (46 to 61 cm.).

Attach the hands of the toy to the stick with long threads, Fig. 151A. Page 14 shows how the toy looks when in action.

An alternative method is to make a cross-bar, Fig. 151B, 9 × 6 in. (15 × 23 cm.) with a metal hook at the top end (this enables toys to be easily stored). Attach all the strings to the cross-bar, Fig. 151C. When in action the cross-bar looks like 151D.

This method of stringing enables a performer of the toys to play with two at the same time.

The toys when moved or raised and lowered to the ground give different sound effects.

The Mini-Lek, Page 46, Plate 10, can perform a slow, gliding movement and give a gentle tinkling sound, but when the pace of movement is quickened by the performer, the toy becomes more active and starts to shoot out its legs. These movements can be regulated to happen with certain sounds of music. In fact, the movement of the Mini-Lek, when he shoots out his four legs with speed, may look as though he is in a temper.

The sound effects are governed by the materials used.

The tinkle of metal is best obtained by using bottle tops of the clip-on variety, or the screw top. By arranging for several of these tops to be on top of each other, then the sound is obtained when the group is raised and lowered.

84

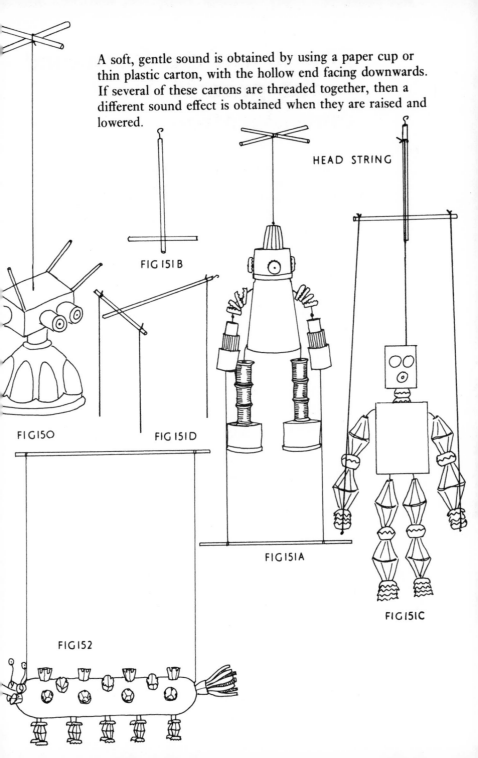

A soft, gentle sound is obtained by using a paper cup or thin plastic carton, with the hollow end facing downwards. If several of these cartons are threaded together, then a different sound effect is obtained when they are raised and lowered.

HEAD STRING

FIG 151B

FIG 150

FIG 151D

FIG 151A

FIG 151C

FIG 152

Music and performance— Some practical considerations

Children will start playing with their performing toys even before the last knot is tied and the paint is dry, for in the child-creator's mind this strange amalgam of disused cartons and bottle-tops will have assumed a character of its own, ready to spring to life.

It is natural for young children to express themselves through music, so suggest that the toy might like to make up a song about itself or dance to a nursery rhyme.[1]

Several toys could join in a singing game[2] such as *Nuts in May*, or the *Mulberry Bush*—in fact, shy children will benefit greatly from sharing toys and taking part in communal activity. Music, however simple, will give a framework to the child's play, which would otherwise have been disorganised and meaningless.

The toys are musical instruments of a sort as they all make a fascinating percussive sound.

Clap a simple rhythm in $\frac{4}{4}$ or $\frac{6}{8}$ time:

e.g. / ♩ ♫ ♩♩ /

and ask the children to get their toys to imitate it. Then repeat the rhythmic pattern four, eight, or sixteen times as the toys dance to it.

Each toy should have its own signature tune. The small ones will skip along in quavers and the long sleeky ones will crawl in minims and semibreves. It would be fun to try to identify each toy by its distinctive musical walk. Some children might get so interested in the sound of their toys that they prefer to drop the strings and concentrate on making musical instruments.[3] In any performance these children could be 'the orchestra' supplying introductory and background music for the toys' activities. It is surprising how much music is just around the place in the average home or school. Get out your tape-recorder and record all the bits and pieces you can find—mother's

86

singing, sister's recorder, aunty's piano, a children's record request programme, excerpts from favourite discs, some home-spun guitar—arrange it into a sequence and you will have a musical patchwork to serve as a backing for the toys to perform to. If you leave spaces for improvised song and speech you will find you have your own 'miniature musical'.

Young people today, with an increasing amount of leisure time, welcome a hobby which demands constructive and interpretative skills. They react so readily to music that they find no difficulty in transferring their own rhythmic responses to the performing toys. With the current move for self-expression through group-music-making of all kinds, the toys should be well served by teenage musicians and poets.

In the classroom situation there are obvious advantages in using gramophone records to stimulate movement, provided the music is immediately attractive to the listener. Excerpts from the following have been used:

Bach:	Brandenburg Concertos
	Swingle Singers
Bizet:	Carmen
	L'Arlésienne Suites
Dvorak:	Slavonic Dances
Grieg:	Peer Gynt Suites
Holst:	The Planets Suite
Mozart:	Eine Kleine Nachtmusik
Prokofiev:	Peter and the Wolf
Purcell:	Trumpet Voluntary
Ravel:	Bolero
Saint-Saens:	Carnival of the Animals
Johann Strauss I:	Radetsky March
Johann Strauss II:	Blue Danube
Stravinsky:	Petrouchka Suite
Tchaikovsky:	Nutcracker Suite
Walton:	Façade Suite
Warlock:	Capriol Suite

In addition, these types of music are very suitable:

Dance Music:[4]	Old Time, Modern and National (Scottish Reels, Latin-American, Calypsos, Jamaican Rumbas, Russian Cossack Dances, etc.).

87

Dramatised Stories:[5]
Electronic Music—this has the advantage of sounding
disembodied, rather like these space-age
toys.
Military Music —Colonel Bogey for a group!
Music and Movement Records:[6]
Jazz:
Pop: —but be careful to use only current
numbers.

Children will display astonishing ingenuity in constructing
toys and their creative powers should be still further
exercised when they play with them. Whatever music is
used, it must not be allowed to stifle children's ideas.
Rather it should be the touchstone for happy and
imaginative play. From the nursery school to the youth
centre and beyond, these simple performing toys will give
endless pleasure.

IAN SHARP

1. *The Oxford Nursery Song Book*   O.U.P.
2. *The Clarendon Books of Singing Games I and II* O.U.P.
3. *Musical Instruments Made to be Played*   DRYAD PRESS,
   Ronald Roberts   LEICESTER
4. See the current E.M.I. catalogue, *Folk and
   Traditional Dances*
5. See the current E.M.I. catalogue, *Records for the
   Primary School*
6. See the current E.M.I. catalogue, *Listen, Move and Dance*

E.M.I. CATALOGUES, BUT NOT THE ACTUAL RECORDS, ARE AVAILABLE FROM:
E.M.I. Records
Education Dept. (P.O. Box No. 1ES)
20 Manchester Square
London W1A 1ES

AMERICAN RECORD COMPANIES WHICH ISSUE CATALOGUES OF CHILDREN'S
RECORDS OF RHYTHMS:

Bowmer Records
622 Radear Drive
Glendale California

RCA Victor Educational Sales
Records for Education
155 E. 24 Street
New York New York 10010

Stanbow Records
Valhalla
New York

Folkways-Scholastic
906 Sylvan Avenue
Englewood Cliffs New Jersey 07632

Educational Record Sales
157 Chambers Street
New York New York 10007

Listening Library
1 Park Avenue
Old Greenwich Conn. 06870

Miss Cube and Mr. Tweedy looking very
apprehensive at Miss Triangle's downfall.

Mathematical bouncing toys

The shape of these toys is inspired from looking at various mathematical shapes, Fig. 153. The shapes may be used to design figures which are flat; by using two pieces of fabric and stuffing, the shape then produces a three-dimensional

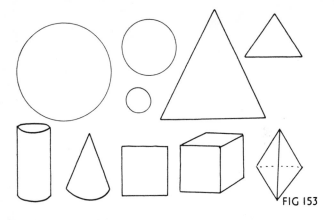

FIG 153

toy. The toy on Plate 26 is based on the use of a cone and the body is hollow to give a more effective figure for movement.

The toys are basically made of felt and a great deal of the character of the toy is obtained from the facial expression. It will be seen from the ideas given in Fig. 154A to 154H, how quickly facial expression can be obtained. It is best to use rounded shapes for a rounded face, or angular shapes, Fig. 154F, for a face of angular design, e.g. Miss Triangle, Plate 25.

In the toys described, the colours and fabrics given are those used for the original, but, of course, you may prefer to try others.

The bouncing of the toys is obtained by attaching a piece of shirring elastic to the top of the toy. If, when the elastic is held, the toy will not bounce, then it is too light in weight. Put a little shot, or small pieces of metal or lead, inside the stuffing of the toy.

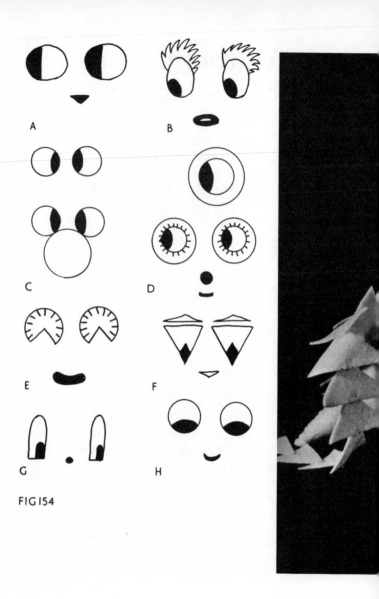

A

B

C

D

E

F

G

H

FIG 154

Plate 19   Miss Cube, Miss Bright Eye and Flying Fish

Mr. Clown

Materials required
$5\frac{1}{2} \times 4\frac{1}{2}$ in. (12×14 cm.) black felt.
$7\frac{1}{2} \times 10\frac{1}{2}$ in. (19×26.5 cm.) check fabric, which does not fray.
$2\frac{1}{2} \times 3$ in. (7.5×8 cm.) white felt. Scrap of red felt.
Kapok for stuffing.

Pattern
Trace off the pattern from Fig. 155.

Cutting out
1. Cut out two legs and two arms in the black felt, Fig. 156.
2. Cut out two body pieces in check fabric. Fig. 157.
3. Trace off the pattern of the face from the body and cut out the face in white felt.
4. Cut out two edge-of-arm pieces in white felt. The one side cut with pinking shears to give a decorative effect, Fig. 158A and B.

To make
1. Place the white face over the body and join with small stitches, Fig. 159.
2. Using the scraps of black felt, cut out eyes and eyebrows the same shape as in Fig. 161 and stick on to face.
3. Trace off the nose pattern from Page 94 and cut out two pieces in red felt. Join the two pieces together by oversewing (firmly overcasting) and stuff firmly before finally completing the stitching, Fig. 160.
4. Stitch nose on to face and use chain stitch for mouth and stem stitch for the side curves of the mouth, Fig. 161.
5. Join the two body sections together by oversewing (firmly overcasting), and stuff firmly.
6. Stitch on the black legs as in Fig. 162.
7. Stick a strip of white felt, Fig. 158A to edge of arm, Fig. 163.
8. Stitch arms to body at point A of pattern, Fig. 155.
9. Secure a piece of shirring elastic to top of head.

Plate 20   Mr. Clown
in action

PATTERN

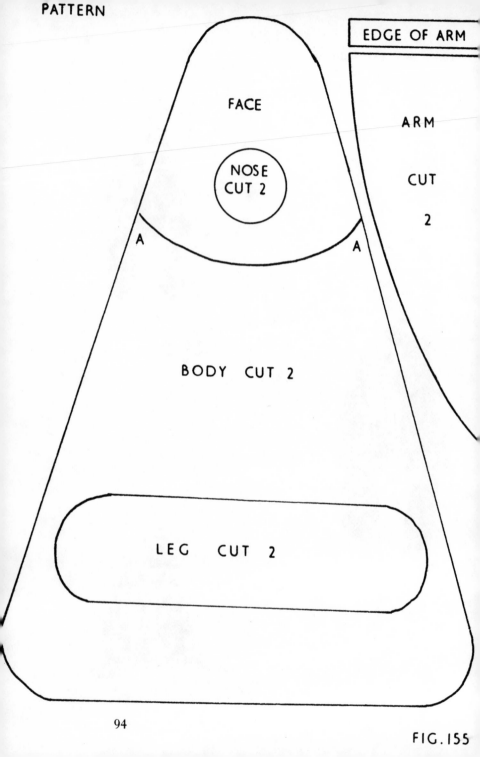

EDGE OF ARM

FACE

ARM

NOSE
CUT 2

CUT

2

A   A

BODY   CUT   2

LEG   CUT   2

94

FIG. 155

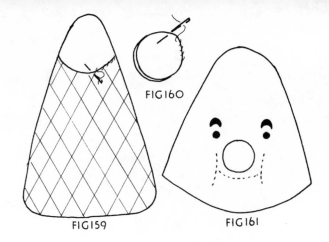

FIG 160

FIG 159

FIG 161

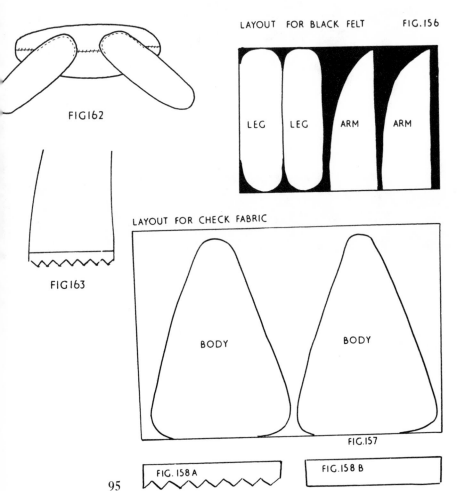

FIG 162

FIG 163

LAYOUT FOR BLACK FELT   FIG.156

LEG   LEG   ARM   ARM

LAYOUT FOR CHECK FABRIC

BODY   BODY

FIG.157

FIG.158 A

FIG.158 B

Plate 21   Mr. Spider in benign and sinister moods

Mr. Spider

Materials required
6 × 12 in. (16 × 31 cm.) orange felt.
3 × 1½ in. (4 × 8 cm.) white felt.
6 × 6½ in. (16 × 17 cm.) black felt.
Kapok for stuffing.
Shirring elastic.
Eight pipe cleaners.

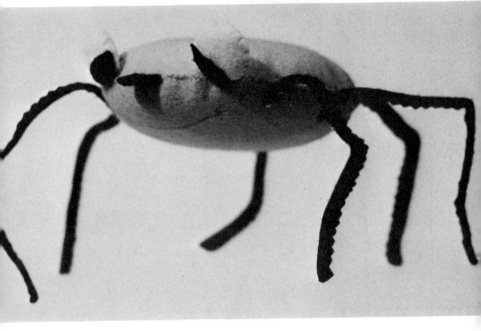

Pattern Trace off the pattern from Fig. 164.

Cutting out
1. Cut out two head pieces in orange felt, Fig. 166.
2. Cut out eight legs, using pinking shears (or cut out straight and cut notches in the felt like those made by pinking shears), Fig. 165.
3. Cut out two dark eye-sections from the black felt, also a tongue, Fig. 165.
4. Cut out two white circles for eyes.

97

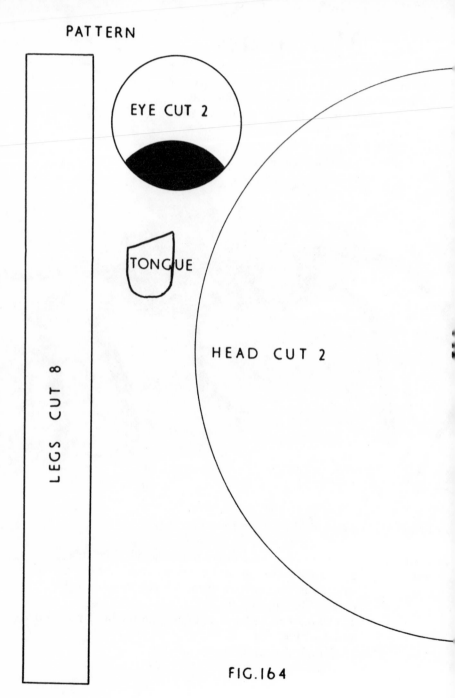

PATTERN

EYE CUT 2

TONGUE

LEGS CUT 8

HEAD CUT 2

FIG. 164

98

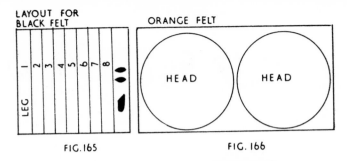

LAYOUT FOR BLACK FELT

LEG

1 2 3 4 5 6 7 8

ORANGE FELT

HEAD

HEAD

FIG. 165

FIG. 166

To make up

Place the two orange-coloured circles together and join by firm overcasting, Fig. 167. Before completing, stuff firmly with kapok.

To make the eyes, place one black eye-piece on top of a white circle and running-stitch together, Fig. 168.

Place on top of white circle and oversew, Fig. 169. Stuff firmly before completing.

Make a second eye.

Stitch on the lower part of the two eyes, to give a facial expression, as in Fig. 170, and stitch on tongue, Fig. 171. Make the legs by covering the pipe cleaners with felt, Fig. 172. Stitch legs to underside of body, Fig. 173, and bend into position. Make him look creepy. Attach a length of shirring elastic to top of head by putting a knot into the end of elastic and catch to head with two or three stitches, using ordinary sewing cotton.

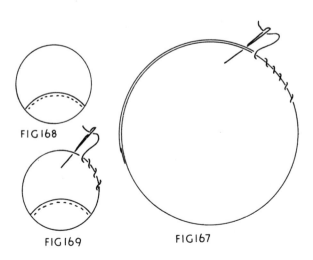

FIG 168

FIG 169

FIG 167

99

FIG 170

FIG 171

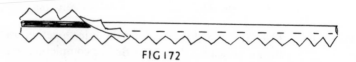

FIG 172

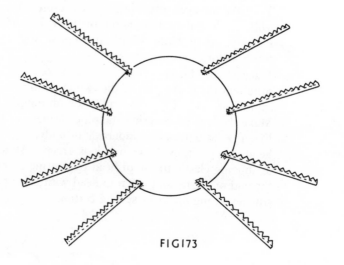

FIG 173

Miss Cube

Plate 22   Miss Cube

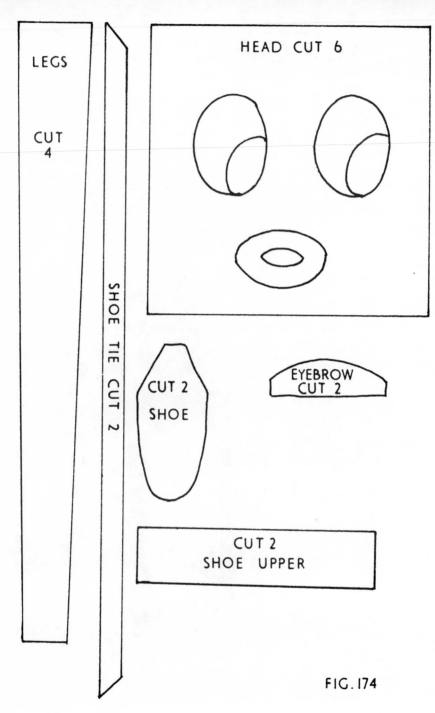

LEGS

CUT
4

SHOE TIE CUT 2

HEAD CUT 6

CUT 2
SHOE

EYEBROW
CUT 2

CUT 2
SHOE UPPER

FIG. 174

102

Materials required

6 × 9 in. (16 × 23 cm.) orange felt.
6½ × 3 in. (17 × 7·5 cm.) grey felt.
4¼ × 2 in. (11 × 5 cm.) green felt.
9 × ½ in. (23 × 1·5 cm.) purple felt.
Scrap of white and black felt. Kapok. Ball of yellow wool.
Shirring elastic.

Pattern

Trace off the pattern from Fig. 174. (Note: Fig. 175 shows layout only, and is not the right size for tracing.)

Cutting out

1. Mark out six squares on to the orange felt and cut out.
2. Mark out four legs on to the grey felt and cut out.
3. Using the green felt mark out two shoe uppers and two shoes. Cut out.
4. Using the purple felt mark out two purple eyes (dark portion in Fig. 175) and two shoe tie pieces. Cut out.
5. Cut out two large white eyes from white felt.

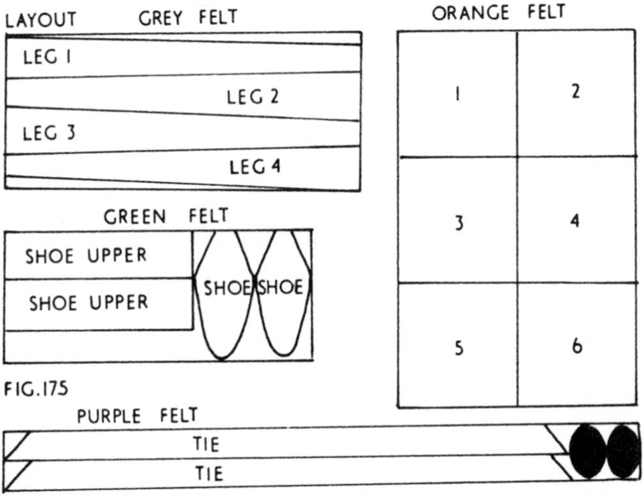

FIG.175

To make up the face

1. Place purple eye on to white eye and stitch, Fig. 176A and B.
2. Using one square for the face, place the eyes into position and stitch. Fig. 177.
3. Cut out a mouth in black felt and stitch on to face, Fig. 178.
4. Cut out two eyebrows in black felt, using pattern opposite. Cut down from top edge to form a fringe (eye

lashes), Fig. 179A and B. Stitch on to the eye as in
Fig. 180A and continue until it looks like Fig. 180B.

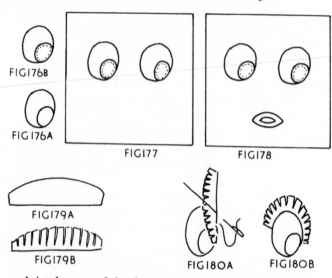

FIG176B

FIG176A

FIG177

FIG178

FIG179A

FIG179B

FIG180A

FIG180B

To make
up the
head

1. Join the top of the face to one square and oversew
(overcast firmly) together, Fig. 181.
2. Join on three more squares as in Fig. 182.
3. Fold down the sides and stitch to form a cube, Fig. 183.
4. Turn upside down and stitch on the remaining square,
and before completing the stitching, stuff, Fig. 184.

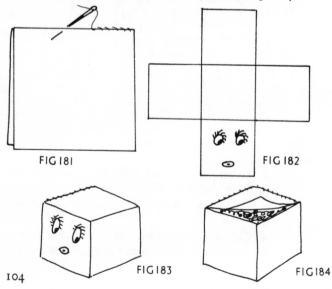

FIG181

FIG182

FIG183

FIG184

Making the legs

1. Place two leg pieces together and join by oversewing, (firm overcasting). Fig. 185.
2. Join shoe pieces to upper, Fig. 186A and B.
3. Secure the leg inside shoe.
4. Stitch up the shoe, Fig. 187.
5. Make a bow of purple felt and stitch in position, Fig. 188.
6. Stitch legs on to underside of cube, Fig. 189.

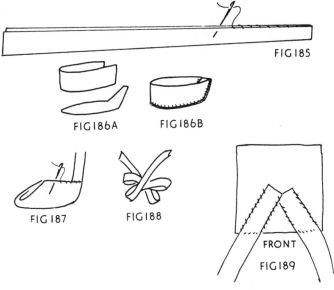

FIG 185

FIG 186A   FIG 186B

FIG 187   FIG 188

FRONT
FIG 189

Making the hair

1. Cut a piece of cardboard 5½ (14 cm.) by 2 in. (0·5 cm.).
2. Wind the yellow wool around the card many times, cut as indicated by arrow and tie on top, Fig. 190A, B and C.
3. Place on to top of cube and stitch, Fig. 191.
4. Secure a piece of shirring elastic to centre of hair on cube.

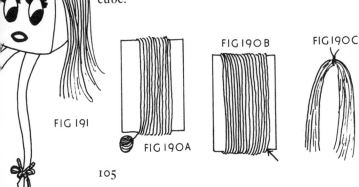

FIG 191

FIG 190B   FIG 190C

FIG 190A

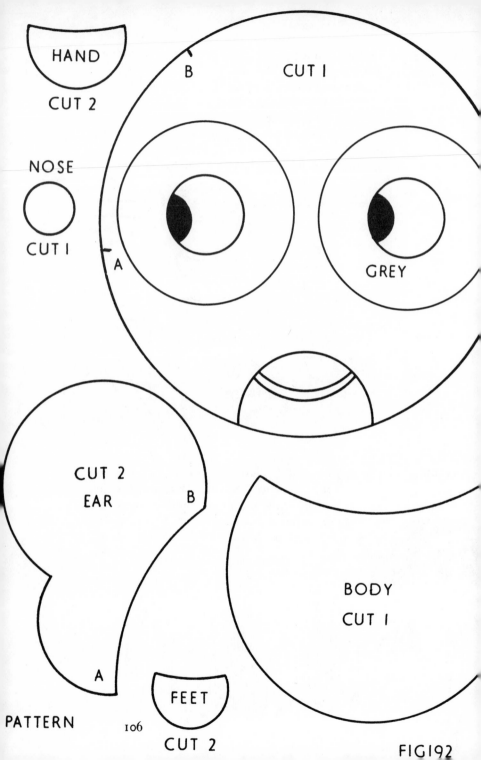

HAND
CUT 2

NOSE

CUT 1

B

CUT 1

GREY

A

CUT 2
EAR

B

BODY
CUT 1

A

PATTERN   106   FEET
CUT 2

FIG192

Mr. Tweedy

Plate 23   Mr. Tweedy

Materials 7×9 in. (18×23 cm.) yellow felt.
required 3×3 in. (8×8 cm.) yellow and black tweed.
$4 \times 2\frac{1}{2}$ in. (10×7 cm.) grey felt.
$5 \times 3\frac{1}{2}$ in. (12×9 cm.) white felt.
Scraps of red felt.
Scraps of black felt.
Kapok.
Shirring elastic.

Pattern   Trace off the pattern from Fig. 192 and Fig. 193. Fig. 194 is a layout diagram only.

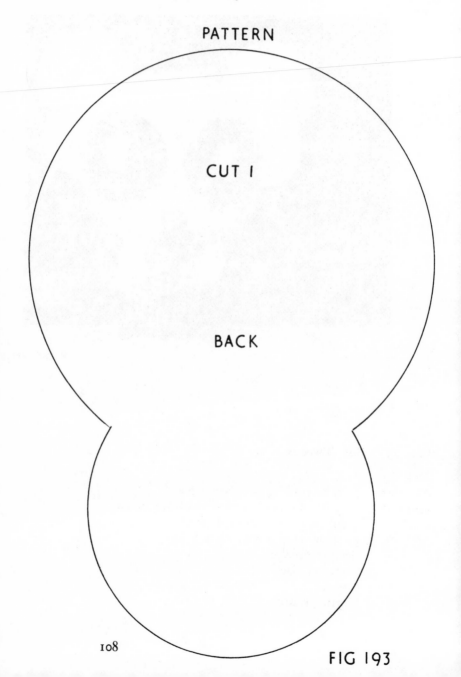

PATTERN

CUT 1

BACK

FIG 193

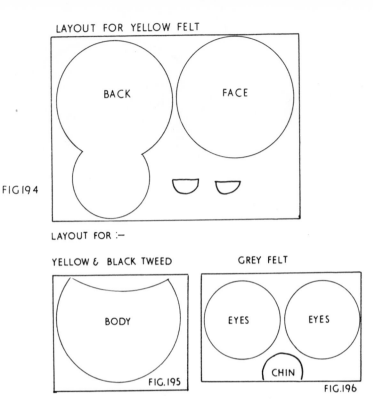

LAYOUT FOR YELLOW FELT

BACK

FACE

FIG 194

LAYOUT FOR :—

YELLOW & BLACK TWEED

BODY

FIG.195

GREY FELT

EYES   EYES

CHIN

FIG.196

LAYOUT FOR :—

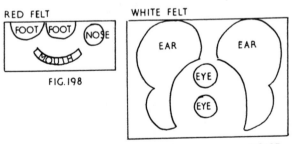

RED FELT

FOOT FOOT NOSE

MOUTH

FIG.198

WHITE FELT

EAR   EAR

EYE

EYE

FIG 197

Cutting out 1. Using the yellow felt, mark out one face and one back section, plus two hand-pieces, and cut out, Fig. 194.
2. Using the tweed, cut out one body piece, Fig. 195.
(If the tweed frays back it with iron-on stiffening.)
3. Use the grey fabric and cut out two large eyes and one chin, Fig. 196.
4. Cut remaining pieces in the white and the red as shown in Figs. 197 and 198.

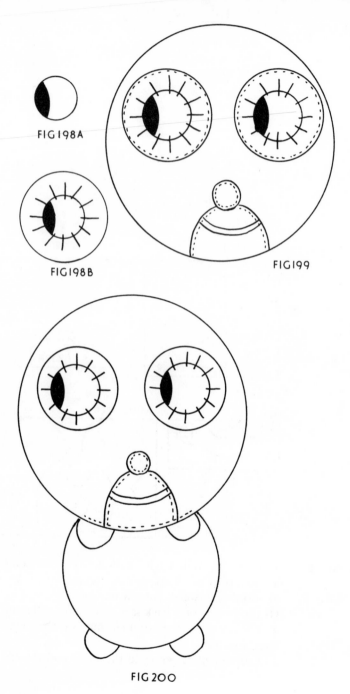

FIG198A

FIG198B

FIG199

FIG200

To make   1. Put the black eye section on to the white circle, Fig. 198A, and run-stitch.

2. Place the white circle on to the grey, Fig. 198B, and use long black stitches to hold it in place. Make a second eye.

3. Place the eye on to the face and hold in place with running stitches, Fig. 199.

4. Stitch on the grey chin, red mouth and red nose, Fig. 199, and stitch on the yellow hands.

5. Join the head and body together, Fig. 200, and put on the red feet.

6. Place the ear pieces into position, matching the markings A and B of ear to A and B of head, and tack. Join the head and body to the back section, and running-stitch together. Before completing, stuff firmly with kapok.

7. Attach a piece of shirring elastic to top of head.

Plate 24   Flying Fish

112

Flying Fish

Except for the eyes, this fish is made up entirely of triangles.

Materials required
5 × 7 in. (13 × 18 cm.) yellow felt.
Scrap of black and white felt.
Kapok for stuffing.
Shirring elastic.

Pattern
Trace off the pattern, Fig. 201A, B, C and D.

Cutting out
Cut out two pieces for the body and 20 pieces for the tail, all in yellow felt. Fig. 202 shows the cutting layout.
Cut out two large eye pieces in black felt and two small pieces in white.

To make
1. Oversew (overcast) the two body pieces together and stuff firmly, Fig. 203. The body should be weighted to give bounce, so put in a few pieces of shot, ball-bearings or anything small to add weight. Attach the shirring elastic to one corner and see if the toy will bounce.
2. Stick on the black and white pieces for eyes and make a couple of stitches for mouth, Fig. 204.
3. Join the tail pieces by overlapping each section, making two long tails each of ten pieces, Fig. 205.
4. Stitch a tail section to each side of the body, Fig. 206. The finished toy should look like Plate 24. The long tail pieces float about as the toy is bounced up and down.

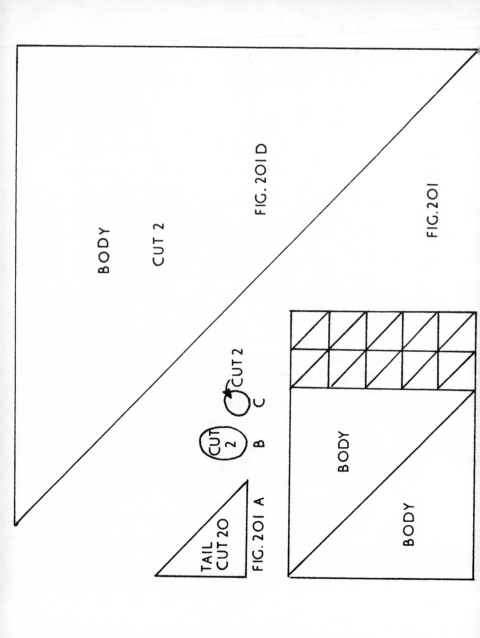

BODY

CUT 2

FIG. 201 D

FIG. 201

CUT 2

C

CUT 2

B

TAIL
CUT 20

FIG. 201 A

BODY

BODY

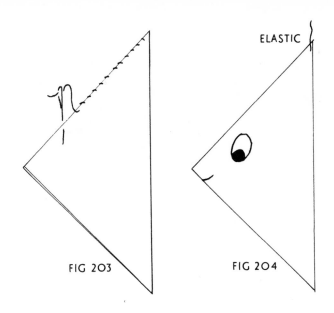

FIG 203   FIG 204

ELASTIC

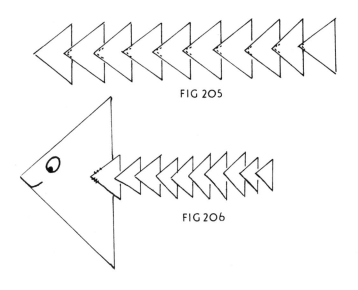

FIG 205

FIG 206

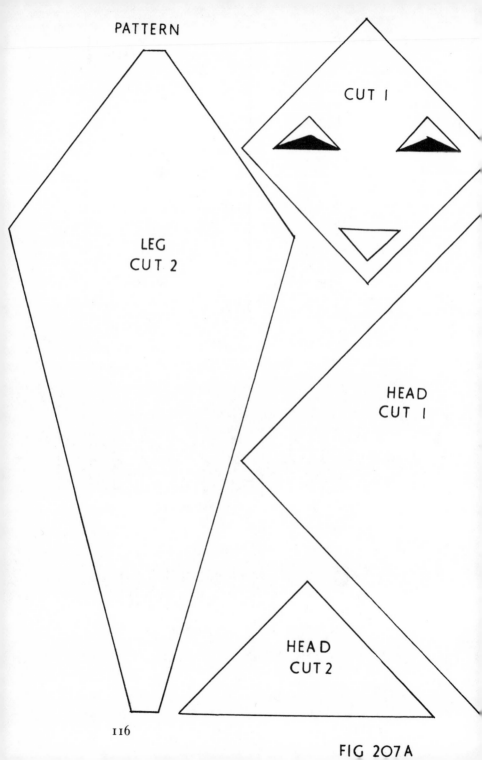

PATTERN

CUT I

LEG
CUT 2

HEAD
CUT I

HEAD
CUT 2

116

FIG 207 A

Miss Triangle

Materials required
$7\frac{1}{2} \times 8$ in. (19×21 cm.) orange felt.
$2\frac{1}{2} \times 2\frac{1}{2}$ in. (6×6 cm.) yellow felt.
$1\frac{1}{2} \times 4$ in. (4×10 cm.) black felt.
Odd scraps of white felt.
Pipe cleaners.

Pattern
Trace off the pattern from Fig. 207A and B.

To make
1. Using the yellow square for the face, attach the black mouth and the white eyes. Then add the black centres. A long black stitch is used to extend the eyes, Figs. 209 and 210.

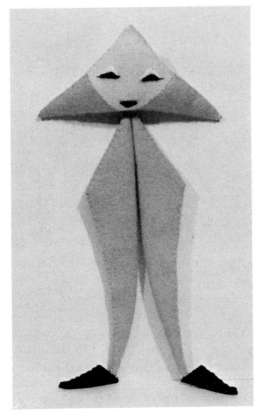

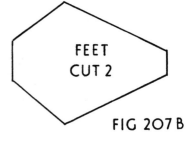

FEET
CUT 2

FIG 207 B

Plate 25 **Miss Triangle**

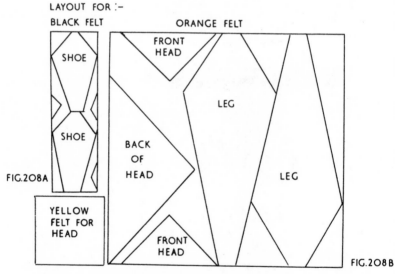

LAYOUT FOR :-

BLACK FELT

ORANGE FELT

SHOE

FRONT HEAD

LEG

SHOE

BACK OF HEAD

LEG

FIG.208A

YELLOW FELT FOR HEAD

FRONT HEAD

FIG.208B

2. Place the front-head piece over the face and stitch along one side, Fig. 210.

3. Open out and attach the second face-piece to the other half of face, Fig. 211.

4. Open out flat and place on top of the back head piece and oversew (overcast firmly) together, Fig. 212. Before completing, stuff firmly with kapok.

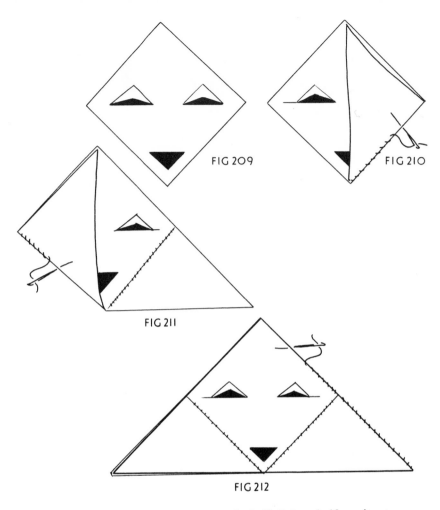

FIG 209

FIG 210

FIG 211

FIG 212

5. Cut one pipe-cleaner in half. Join a half-section to one end of an uncut pipe-cleaner, Fig. 213A.

6. Attach the pipe-cleaner down the centre of leg, Fig. 213B.

7. Fold leg-piece over and join by oversewing (firm overcasting), Fig. 213C.

8. Bend foot outwards and attach black shoe. Make a second leg, Fig. 213D.

9. Attach legs to centre of lower edge of head triangle.

10. Attach shirring elastic to top of head.

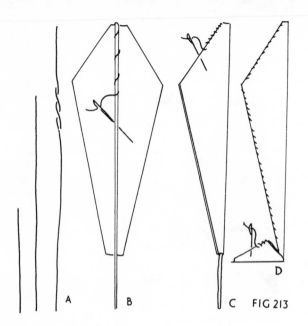

A   B   C   FIG 213   D

Miss Trews

Plate 26   Miss Trews

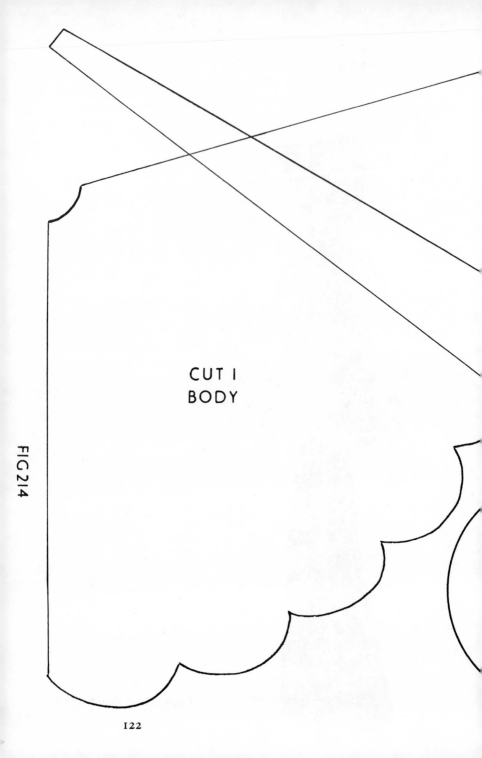

CUT 1
BODY

FIG 214

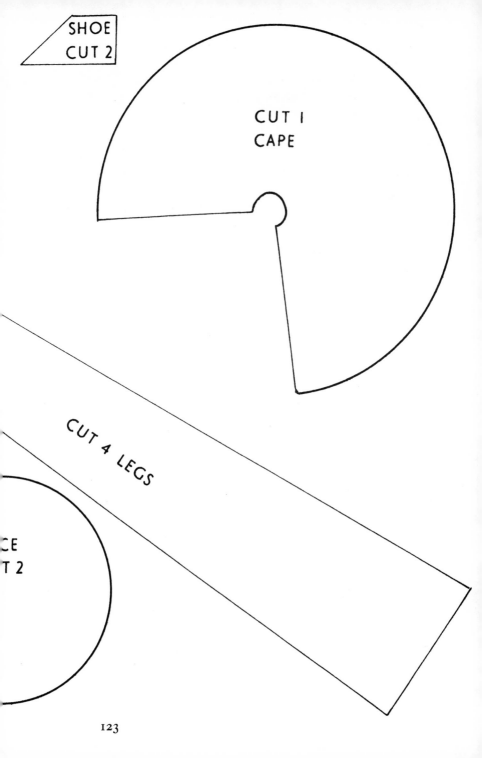

SHOE
CUT 2

CUT 1
CAPE

CUT 4 LEGS

CE
T 2

123

Materials	10 × 12 in. (26 × 30 cm.) black felt.
required	10 × 7 in. (26 × 18 cm.) orange felt.
	Scrap of white felt.
	Kapok for stuffing.
	Half a pipe cleaner.

Pattern   Trace off the pattern from Figs. 214 and 216.

Cutting out 1. See chart, Fig. 215A. Cut out in the black felt four legs, two arms, one cape and one head cover.
2. Using the orange felt cut out one body, two faces, two hands and two feet, Fig. 215B.

LAYOUT FOR BLACK FELT

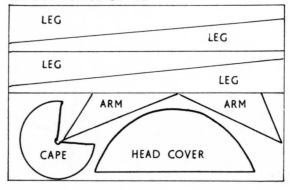

FIG 215A

LAYOUT FOR ORANGE FELT

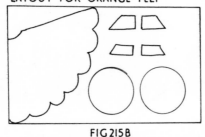

FIG 215B

To make   1. Stitch on an orange foot to each leg, Fig. 217A and B.
2. Place two leg-pieces together and join with running stitch, Fig. 218.
3. Join body by oversewing (firm overcasting), Fig. 219.

124

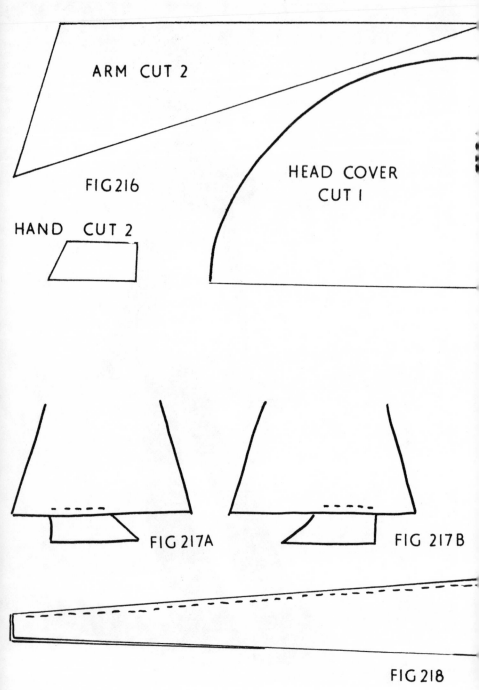

ARM CUT 2

FIG 216

HAND CUT 2

HEAD COVER
CUT 1

FIG 217A

FIG 217B

FIG 218

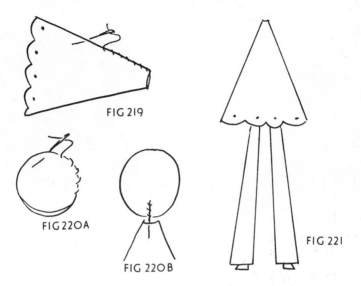

FIG 219

FIG 220A

FIG 220B

FIG 221

4. Attach legs to neck of body, Fig. 221.
5. Join head pieces together by oversewing, and stuff; also insert half of the pipe cleaner up into the head and down into the body, Fig. 220A and B. Secure head to top edge of body.
6. Join hands on to lower edge of arms, and join arms to neck of body, Figs. 222 and 223.

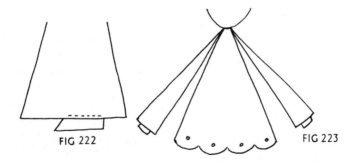

FIG 222

FIG 223

7. Wrap cape around top of body and join edges together at back.
8. Stick on features in black and white felt.
9. Put on head-cover and attach under chin.
10. Attach shirring elastic to top of head.

127

Plate 27   Miss Bright Eye

Miss Bright-Eye

Materials required
12 × 5 in. (30 × 13 cm.) bright flame-coloured felt.
6 × 6 in. (15 × 15 cm.) light-blue fabric which will not fray.
Scrap of white and scrap of black felt.
Kapok.
Bonded fabric 6 × 6 in. (15 × 15 cm.) for stiffening (iron-on).

Pattern
Trace off the pattern on Page 130, and use the leg pattern of Miss Trews on Page 123. Divide this leg pattern into two lengthwise, making the legs long and thin.

Cutting out
1. See chart, Fig. 225 and cut out four legs, two heads and two arms in flame-coloured felt.
2. Cut out the body and ears in light-blue fabric, Fig. 226. Back the body with the bonded fabric.

LAYOUT FOR FLAME COLOURED FELT.

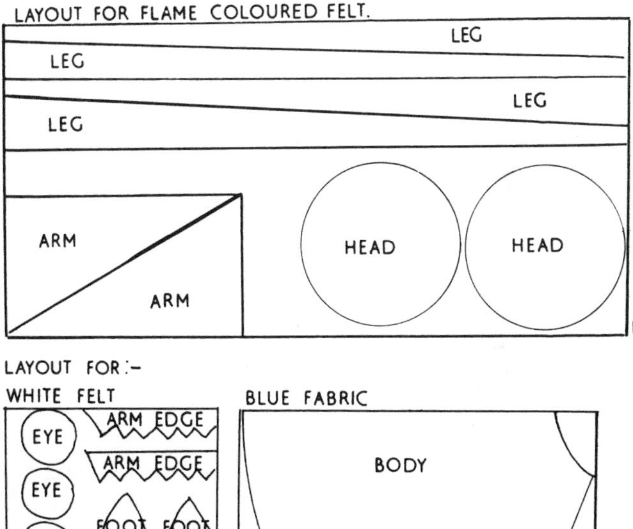

LEG
LEG
LEG
LEG
ARM
ARM
HEAD
HEAD

FIG.225

LAYOUT FOR :–

WHITE FELT

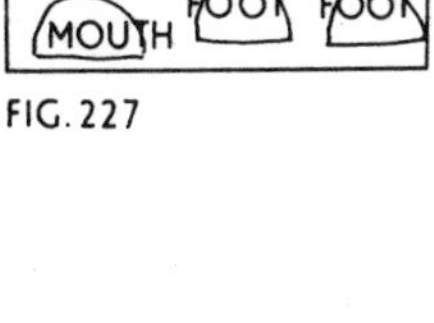

EYE
ARM EDGE
ARM EDGE
EYE
MOUTH
FOOT FOOT

FIG.227

BLUE FABRIC

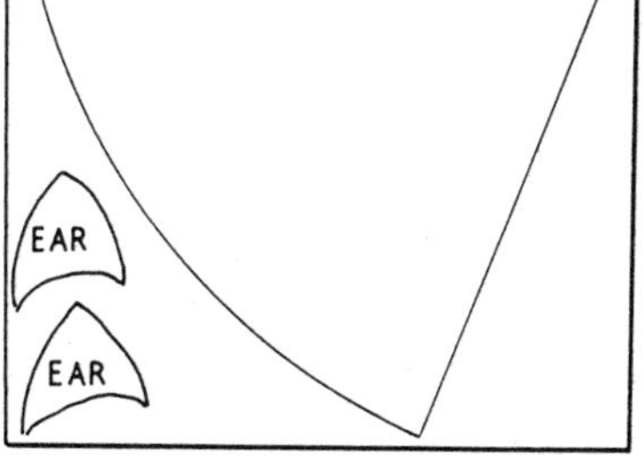

BODY

EAR
EAR

129   FIG.226

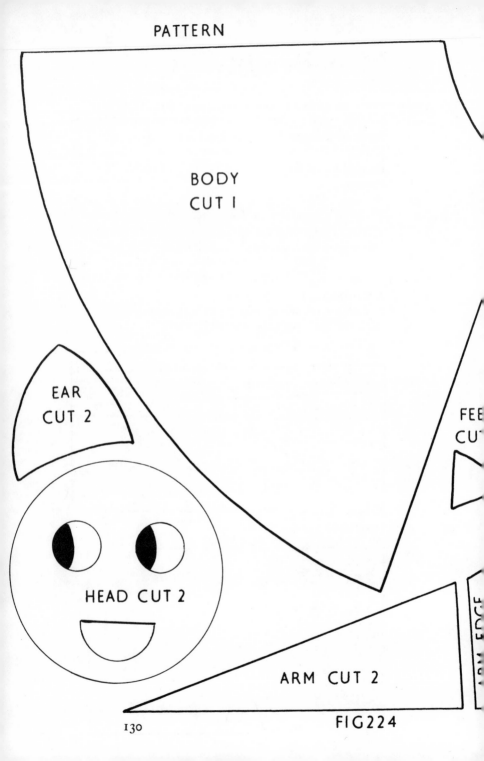

PATTERN

BODY
CUT 1

EAR
CUT 2

FEE[...]
CU[...]

HEAD CUT 2

ARM CUT 2

ARM EDGE

130

FIG 224

3. Cut out white shoes, arm-bands, eyes and mouth, Fig. 227.

To make Follow instructions for the making of Miss Trews on Page 124, but attach ears to head to complete the toy.